Glooed

Glooed

by

Jeanne M. Carroll

Library of Congress Control Number: 2018910656

Print ISBN   978-1-7326249-0-0
ebook ISBN   978-1-7326249-1-7

Book design and layout by Amanda Rodriguez
Chapter Illustrations: Franklin D. Robinson, IV

Glooed is dedicated to the memory of Joseph Marion McLaughlin, my mom's father, my granddad, who sang the praises of writing in plain and simple words. According to Granddad, the secret to good writing is rewriting, not once or twice but as many times as is necessary to achieve flow and a crystal-clear message. I have tried to follow his advice by rewriting obsessively, to the chagrin of those who helped me finalize *Glooed*. Since Granddad did not live nearby, I did not see him often. We had a long-distance relationship built on written communication and sustained by his persistent and constant desire to be involved in my life. He was my cheerleader, teacher, and critic highlighting the incredible influence a grandparent can have on a child.

Acknowledgments

I set out to write a book about my grandkids for my grandkids. I ended up writing a book about me, perhaps for me. The grandkids figure largely in this book as their arrival was a catalyst in the changing direction of my life. In addition to the grands, there are many to acknowledge in the completion of Glooed. First, I thank my sister, Patti Fullen. Patti walked the Oakland Hills with me in spirit when my granddaughter was a baby and I was out of my mind. She then became a passenger on my drive home from Oakland each week. I called her often, recounting the adventures of the day. She empathized with my experiences, recounted some of her own, laughed with me as we considered our maladies, genetic and otherwise, and encouraged me to put it all in writing.

My very talented niece, Amanda Rodriguez, prepared the manuscript for publication and coordinated the progress of the illustrations and the text. She managed me and the changes that I seemed to make hourly with a smile. It was an honor to work with this very capable woman whom I have known since she was a toddler. Amanda's equally talented brother and my nephew, Franklin D. Robinson IV, drew the illustrations. Having this kind of help from the used-to-be littles is truly coming full circle.

Finally, where would I be without family and more, who would I be? I was molded by family experiences and then turned around and grew my own family. My siblings are a comfort for the most part: Life would be boring and lonely without them. My husband, Patrick, has stood by me and loved me even when I have been less than loveable. My children were my life until the grands arrived. In truth they are still my life. No one is more important than parents – they shape us by what they do and do not do, by what they say and do not say – while my grandparents figured oh so prominently in my development and in how I conduct myself today.

Introduction

Getting old can be exciting, traumatic or seemingly unattainable depending upon the age being celebrated. I was never much affected by my birthday, not at 18 or 50. The mirror looked the same to me, when I would dare to look. That all changed in my 60's, and to be precise, when I was 61. My hip failed me – and I suddenly felt and looked every year of my being. Walking across the street became hazardous, not sure that I would make it before a car slowly approaching from one-half mile away was upon me. Getting through a day of teaching eighth graders became painful – not for the reasons some might think. I loved teaching, but I could no longer easily glide between the desks and engage in fun labs. At night, I began parking on the rocking chair and falling asleep with my mouth unattractively agape. I slept fitfully – awakened throughout the night by my sore hip, which cried out for a new position.

Orthopedic specialists advised me that I needed a hip replacement, a surprising turn of events as I prided myself on being active throughout my life. Little did I know that an active lifestyle might be good for the heart, but a death knell for one's joints. Up until that point, I had not seriously considered retiring. Teaching was stimulating, active, and challenging, but this hip failure had me considering it right then and there.

I could not imagine life without that pain and as it turns out, my family had other ideas for me as well, which tipped the scale in favor of retirement. At 61 years and seven months, I retired, underwent hip replacement surgery, and completely and utterly changed the course of my life. I have been adjusting ever since.

1

A PASS

I retired at the end of May 2016 and had hip surgery that June. Five days before surgery, my daughter threw me a surprise retirement party. I am not a gracious receiver, not of gifts, compliments, or parties. It was a surprise for sure.

Many of my co-workers were there, as well as family members. I felt as awkward as one could feel. It reminded me of the time my aunt and sister Deb threw me a 15th birthday party. They invited a handful of people (all girls) that they thought were my friends. I knew them, but they were not really friends. I was an awkward teenager and did not have many friends. They invited one "special friend" to spend the night, although she was no such thing. I was a loner in many ways and having a party was painful – a party where I was responsible for people overnight was excruciating. The next morning when I awoke, I peeked into the guest bedroom where my "friend" was staying and saw her sitting on the edge of the bed fully clothed and ready to go. It was only 6 o'clock! That was one of the longest mornings of my life. I thought for sure I would never be in such a position again. Ironically, my sister Deb was involved in this shindig as well – she apparently never got the memo that she had ruined my life when I was 15.

This party was a little different. I liked everyone that was invited. I knew they all had good intentions and there was beer. But, I was not happy about this retirement thing and a celebration was the furthest thing from my mind. I literally limped through the night and prepared for the next big event, hip replacement surgery.

The surgery and my retirement are inextricably intertwined. I cannot think of one without thinking of the other. For the first month after surgery, I had no thoughts about what I would do next. Since retirement began at school's end, I was on a natural break from school anyway. Because this hip issue arose so quickly, I really had not constructed a life-after-work plan.

Additionally, I was snowed by pain medication the first few weeks after surgery. I spent hours watching shows on Netflix, sitting in a comfy leather rocking chair, dressed in a "moo moo" (a long nightie gown for old women) with drool streaming down my chin. Despite all of the time on Netflix, I could not later remember the substance of any show I had watched.

I am convinced I must have been sleeping with my eyes open. My family gave me a pass from any and all kinds of work that first month and much of the second – and I gave them some respite from me. It was the last time I would ever be so quiet, sedate, and accepting of my lot.

2

BOTHERED BY ME

When I awoke from my medicated slumber, I was faced with the very large question of what to do with the rest of my life. Since I had no plan, I began with cleaning the house. I did that regularly anyway, but now I cleaned more frequently. I had an unwritten policy to cause no harm when I cleaned, so I tried to clean when my kids and their children were not around. It was kind of pointless anyway. However, with so much time on my hands, that policy fell by the wayside. It really had no effect on anyone but me – just frustrated me that bodies were always in the way.

I began to pick at myself more than ever. I was in a bike accident when I was 26 and broke five of my top teeth including the two front ones. Prior to that time, I had a space between those two teeth, inherited from my father's side of the family. I never had a problem with that space, but dentists seemed to, as did my parents apparently. When I was in the eighth grade I was sent to an oral surgeon who cut the gum between the two front teeth and then to an orthodontist who put braces on my imperfect smile to push those teeth together. It was a wasted remedy ultimately as the space returned once the braces were removed. The only thing that fixed that space for good was the bike accident.

I have always had a thing about my teeth. I took very good care of them in an era when there was no such thing as fluoride or floss. The damage done by the bike accident was fairly traumatic as a consequence. Over the years I had root canals as the teeth failed, crowns, and replacement crowns. The replacement teeth could never look like my original teeth because the space was omitted.

Since retirement, I have been somewhat obsessed with those teeth, and the front teeth in particular. Right before my hip surgery, I had new crowns put on. The old crowns had metal backings which gave my teeth a lovely gray color. The new crowns were an improvement in the color category, but something about them bothered me. I have spent too much time looking in the mirror and smiling (actually grimacing) trying to figure out what the heck is wrong with them. I recently asked the dentist what he thought – oh, he said, they are a little long. Ha – they may be, but I also think they are a little wide, covering an area that a space used to occupy. I sure do miss that space. Well, I am going to get these darn things shaved a little in length. I know already it will not satisfy me, but maybe by the time I get that done, I will have less time to obsess over myself.

My teeth are not the only feature about which I obsess. My skin is wrinkled and scarred from stuff I could have controlled and stuff I could not. There was the acne that plagued me as a teenager and then the injuries to my face from playing basketball. I loved basketball and played throughout my youth. My husband did not play much until he met me. He was an awkward player, but he worked hard to avoid losing to a girl. We played a lot out in our driveway both before kids and after. Those games could get a little rough and for the neighbors, disturbing.

On two separate occasions, while coming down from a rebound, my chin hit Patrick's hard head causing my front teeth to cut into my lower lip, leaving gashes on the left and right side of my lower lip. Both injuries required stitches. I attribute those incidents to Patrick's clumsy play, of course. I now have lines that run downward on the left and right side of the bottom lip making for a ventriloquist's dream. I have investigated laser surgery, but I am not comfortable with giving up my face to the hands of another and so the image in the mirror continues to bother me. Clearly, I am not aging attractively.

3

BEAUTIFUL

I have never liked the word ugly. I bristle when I hear it. I suppose I dislike the word because I know what it is like to feel ugly. I have five sisters and two brothers. I distinctly remember my dad referring to my sister Colleen as beautiful. Colleen is the oldest girl, blonde, blue-eyed, and yes, beautiful – to this day still beautiful. We had a player piano when I was little and we all knew that the song "The Girl with the Golden Braids" was Colleen's song.

My youngest sister Patti was the apple of everyone's eye. We all thought she was cute and fun, and she has grown up as such. My mother's mother, Mimi, spent a lot of time with my sister Jill and me when we were little. She often sang to us in the car. One of those songs was *It's a Long Way to Tipperary* and she always gave Jill a knowing nod when she sang the phrase "to the sweetest gal I know". Jill was Mimi's sweet, beautiful girl.

My mother was born in the south and was a true "Southern Belle" because she was beautiful, classy, stylish and elegant – and she lost not an ounce of her beauty throughout her long life. My sister Dee, the seventh in line, looked like my mom so no worries for her.

My sister Deb, the third in line, jokes that no one ever called her pretty but Deb did and does have a great and beaming personality – she smiles and the world smiles with her. I never heard anyone refer to a boy as ugly, but my brothers were not likely to be labeled in that way in any event. Of the eight of us, I seemed to be the one who lost out in the looks department.

I was born cross-eyed and to this day my eyes are squirrelly. After two surgical attempts to fix them and a lot of eye muscle exercises, they still do what they want to do. It is anyone's guess who I am looking at because my eyes do their own thing. While the eye dysfunction actually proved to be quite helpful as a teacher, it was anything but when I was young. The kids in middle school called me Clarence the Cross-eyed Lion for a lion whose antics as a cross-eyed animal were explored in a then popular television show.

In the eighth grade, my skin erupted with acne, not just a pimple here or there, but cystic acne characterized by red swollen painful infections that travel deep into the skin. My father, a doctor but anti-doctor when it came to his family, finally gave in to the terrible skin condition by sending me to a dermatologist. I received antibiotics, ultraviolet light treatments and disturbingly, painful pimple popping sessions – none of which helped and some of which actually made the visual worse.

One thing I was always advised to stay away from was face lotion. The dermatologist said it promoted oily skin and thus more acne. I lived by that advice until I was about 45. My husband, the pharmacist, has forever encouraged me to use face lotion – to save my skin from the toll of long sunny California days – but I pretty much stuck to the plan of the whack dermatologist from the 1970's. As a consequence, I wear the scars from acne and the wrinkles of a Shar Pei. My husband by the way has beautiful skin, enriched by years of tender loving care. He is a year younger than I am, but he looks 15 years younger. He has always joked that I robbed the cradle. With each passing year, it seems less of a joke.

Beautiful people have beautiful hair, or so I thought. I knew I would never be beautiful because I had fine thin hair adorned with cowlicks from the crown of my head to the nape of my neck. I had no control over my mop. Through the years I have tried every short hair cut in the book, a few attempts at growing it out, and one perm in my quest for beautiful hair, a quest which has to this day eluded me. At 63, I am now content to stick with the hair style I had when I was three.

In this seventh decade of life, I still struggle to look in the mirror with an accepting eye. I was much more accepting of myself when I worked – or maybe I just did not look in the mirror as often.

As a teacher, I was full of good energy. I was busy, no time to think about myself, and the kids made me laugh, even when that was not their intention. I have had trouble with generating good energy since retiring and so the smiles come slower and less often. They have been replaced by a somewhat ugly temperament – when I am feeling useless, angry, and bored. Feeling ugly on the inside is much more unsettling than feeling ugly on the outside. As I figure out this retirement thing, I know I can be a better person and maybe I can even be beautiful if I just follow the advice of Carole King in the song, *Beautiful*, and wake up every morning with a smile on my face.

4

IF I COULD CRY

Eight little kids running amok was chaotic and loud. My parents did the best they could at the time considering the monsters that we were. Life as one of eight was mostly fun, resulting in a lot of entertaining stories later in life and some curious lifelong consequences.

I can distinctly remember an occasion when I was about three or four that my sister Deb and I were crying. In the hallway of our very small but full house hung a large oval shaped mirror. My dad, who was more than six feet tall, picked us up, turned us towards the mirror, and told us we should not cry because we look ugly when we cry. In my mind's eye I can still see the childhood images of Deb and me in the mirror looking back at us and crying in full force.

That statement had a profound effect on me. I rarely cry. I want to cry sometimes to relieve the pressure in my chest, but something blocks the process. I fear that one day my pent-up tears will cause a flood like in *Alice's Adventures in Wonderland*.

When I was 11, I lost my best friend, Sean. He had cystic fibrosis and was chronically ill his last few years of life. We had moved a month or so prior to his death. In a misguided effort to protect me, my parents did not tell me until a week or so had passed and only after I had badgered them to take me to see Sean. I missed his funeral and more importantly, the opportunity to grieve. I am sure I cried some, but since I am still thinking about it 52 years later, clearly, I did not cry enough.

Ironically, my dad's words had just the opposite effect on my sister Deb. She cries when she is sad, mad, and even sometimes when she is glad. Deb has the most beautiful soulful eyes, perhaps because she has bathed her eyes in spilled tears over the years. Deb is proof positive that crying does not make one ugly, but it is too late to rewire my brain.

When I retired, I was sad but I did not cry. I packed up my classroom quietly, almost surreptitiously, in the month before my last day, rolling stuff out to my car in the early morning hours before anyone else arrived. Piece by piece, I cleared the walls of years of messages and the t-shirts each 8th grade class had signed, in silent sadness. I gave away stuff I thought my colleagues could use, left stuff I thought the teacher replacing me might find useful, all through written not spoken word. I avoided the staff, my department colleagues, and even the students when they asked if it was true I was retiring. I did not want to cry and expose my ugly self. Leaving my classroom behind, empty and lifeless, felt starkly defining, defeating, final.

Intellectually I know there is no shame in crying. Crying is the honest expression of how we feel. Kids cry so easily because they are so honest. If I could cry, maybe I could finally get over my childhood friend's death, maybe I could once and for all accept my retirement and be completely present in what I am doing now, maybe I could begin to find the honesty that my grands (aka grandchildren) wear on their sleeves. If I could cry maybe I would have beautiful eyes like my sister Deb. If only I could cry ....

5

WORK

I feel best when I am working and productive. Parents have a lot to do with that aspect of one's development, I think. Siblings do too. I am the fourth of eight children. We grew up in New England, land of cold snowy winters and beautiful fall colors. The minute the snow began to fall, my dad would call us to man the shovels. We all ran to our stations on command, but I always seemed to be the only one still shoveling 15 minutes later. I grew to enjoy those shovel days. In a family of ten, there is little space for alone time not to mention quiet time. Shoveling became a peaceful respite for me and a way to work out my pent-up frustrations, which I seemed to have even at eight, nine, and ten years of age.

Winter passed, spring sprung and spring cleaning commenced. I learned to enjoy cleaning as well. The whir of the vacuum cleaner was so much more preferable to the cries of my younger siblings. Spring turned to summer and I was awarded the status of honorary boy for all the lifting projects around the house. Fall brought down the colorful leaves that I gladly raked and collected. My siblings were there helping of course, but not for as long or with as much verve. My father praised me for my work, which kept me shoveling and cleaning and lifting and raking. My siblings did not mind: They knew the more work I did the less they had to do.

I loved school as much as I loved the physical work of raking and shoveling. I was good at it. Math came easily to me and my mom helped me to grow into a person who appreciated proper grammar and word choice. My mom would correct my papers. Perhaps it was in those elementary years that I learned to dislike the color red. She was merciless in a quiet way. My dad gave me math problems. I would work them out and come back for more. When aunts and uncles came to town, my dad was sure to brag about my good grades.

I know now that I was programmed to be busy and productive. As an adult, I carried on the tradition. I worked full time with the exception of the year after each of my two children were born. I managed to keep the house clean and the yard neat. I always had at least one dog and sometimes two that also required time and attention, and I learned to do minor plumbing and household jobs when the need arose.

I have had many jobs in my life, but teaching suited me best as it requires non-stop movement and energy. Besides providing a sense of purpose and direction, work also provides a ready excuse from doing what you do not want to do. Having a work ethic is good until you no longer have the usual work.

6

Yippee, have to work!

EXCUSED

Work has been good to me over the years. After college, I worked in a toxicology lab testing blood and other sundry biological samples for drugs.

I was an attorney for many years, tried a few cases, argued many more cases and have had published opinions both in favor of and against my clients. Knowing how the law works is helpful to understanding almost every aspect of life. I enjoyed the process of practicing law, but almost never enjoyed the clients. Many of my clients were attorneys (a large part of my practice involved defending attorneys from claims that they committed malpractice) and it is true what many say about them: Attorneys are shamelessly full of themselves. I also defended the Roman Catholic Church against a negligent supervision claim based on a priest's predatory and fiduciary breach of his position, the molestation of boys over the course of his priesthood. That case broke me, at which time I looked for other avenues of work and decided upon teaching at 42 years of age.

As a child, I was often the spokesperson for my younger brother and sisters when things went awry, a role that has continued into adulthood. Becoming a lawyer was the natural progression for me but having to defend the Church against these egregious acts of a sick perverted priest ran counter to everything I believed in and for which I stood.

What better way to redeem myself than by jumping into the fray with kids, teaching them, listening to them, advocating for them and helping them to stand on their own two feet. In the end, I received as much as I gave my students in good energy and the hope for a better future.

Work stimulated me, paid the bills, gave me a sense of belonging and a life of purpose. I have to admit work conferred another benefit that I often took advantage of, but to which I rarely admitted. Work provided an excuse from doing the things I had no interest in doing. Working meant I was essentially unapproachable during the work week and on the weekends when and if I wanted to be. I missed extended family outings, out of state events and even local birthday parties. My family lives in Massachusetts and I live in California. Working meant I could go home to visit without having to stay too long. No one questioned me when I planned just a four-day visit.

I no longer have that built-in excuse and everyone seems to know it. I hate shopping, but I am the Costco shopper now. When my husband needs a few toys to donate for Christmas, I get the list because I do not work. I absolutely hate the question – what are your plans for today? The only question I may hate more is – What did you do today? I used to say I am working or I worked and that was enough. Now I feel like there is nothing I can say that will make anyone believe that I did anything other than sit on my duff. I often cannot even remember what I did during the course of a day.

My husband wants to travel to Utah to see his mother. It is an hour and a half plane ride, but an eleven-hour car ride and he wants to drive! I can no longer claim I am busy with work. I miss work, yes, but more, I miss the time and space that work provided.

7

Will Mom
retire?
☐ yes
☐ no

ALL IN THE FAMILY

Being productive and of service seem to be themes that have run through my life. I was the number one helper in my family, raking, cleaning – anything but cooking. When I was 11, my family moved from a working-class neighborhood to an upscale one. I hated it from the start. The new house smelled funny. It was so big that every sound was magnified tenfold, and my friends were in the old neighborhood. I was set to start the sixth grade and had looked forward to this grade level forever, as I was finally old enough to wear the orange crossing garb that signified my ability to safely lead the little ones across the street. The move meant a new school, a Polish Catholic school across town in a very poor neighborhood. For reasons unknown to me, my younger brother Greg (then a first grader) and I were the only siblings sent to this school. We took two buses every morning to get there and reversed the trip each afternoon.

The transition from public to private was big enough but more, I was plopped into a culture I knew nothing about and immersed in a language I did not understand. I was taken aback by the poverty of the neighborhood that this new but very old school served. One of the few friends I made there lived in the top apartment of a three-story tenement building with four siblings and her parents. I visited once, at which time I realized that my friend did not have a bedroom. Her mattress was laid out on the living room floor with several others.

To avoid the bully crowd, Greg and I sometimes skipped the first bus and walked downtown to catch the second bus home, on sidewalks littered with trash and filled with unkempt people. That was my first experience with homelessness and hopelessness, and one that stayed with me for life.

After law school, I wanted to work in the public sector to better the lives of others. That never happened because public service jobs were hard to come by at the time and so I worked in a private law firm and defended arrogant attorneys instead.

I went back to the theme of giving when I became a teacher. My first teaching position was in an urban, low income school, where I taught for seven years. I then went on to another middle school a mile or so down the road where the demographics were similar, a very diverse population, an urban setting and a high percentage of students on the free lunch program. I worked there for another twelve years. I was fully engaged in public service, enjoying, inspiring, being inspired, learning from the students, and serving in an area that many shunned.

When retirement reared its ugly head, I knew I would miss the frenetic pace and the service aspect of my job. As I was debating the if-and-when, my husband Patrick pointed out that our daughter Kristen could use some help with her one-year-old. Her husband, Adam, was the primary caregiver. He was also coaching rugby and embarking on a new career teaching high school Biology. Kristen was a nurse practitioner, working full-time.

At the same time, our son Sean and his wife, Jess, were in the midst of building their family. Jess gave birth to a baby girl a week after my hip replacement surgery. They lived in Oakland where a third of their income was dedicated to the right to live in an 800 square foot apartment. They both worked. Sean was a lowly resident putting in 16 plus hour days and Jess was working from home managing student loan programs and taking care of the day-to-day family stuff. Daycare was an expense that would be difficult to bear and they did not want their girl being watched by some stranger in any event. My helpful husband thought retirement was the right thing for me because Sean and Jess could use my help.

Sharing such thoughts with me was one thing, but Patrick shared his plans for me with my family as well. He told Sean not to worry – Mom was retiring and would be down there a couple of times a week to help (they live 90 miles away). He reassured Kristen similarly. One day family and friends actually voted on whether or not I would retire that particular year, the year I ultimately did retire. Many seemed to have a vested interest in my retirement.

I am not the babysitter type. I was not the mainstream mother type and I doubt I am the grandmother type. If I were my children, I would be a little worried about allowing me to care for their precious babies. After all, my children should know better. They grew up watching my predictable volatility in action. I had fits of frustration when they would spill milk on the floor and they witnessed me stab our new kitchen table with metal tongs when I could not stand listening to them argue anymore. The gouge on that table is still there 20 plus years later. I can see their surprised faces in my mind's eye when the tongs smashed into the table – and hear the laughter that followed, reverberating throughout the kitchen. To even consider me as a caretaker had to be sheer desperation on their part or wanton and reckless disregard for the well-being of their children.

Needless to say, the family's plan won out. I retired, had the surgery, and after a few months of rest and rehabilitation, I began my new job taking care of grandkids. I guess you could say I am fulfilling my goal of serving others – my daughter and her husband, my son and his wife, and my grandkids. I worry that this does not really count since it is all in the family kind of stuff. Nonetheless, I am trying to do my job as well as I can, with as few meltdowns as possible, and with the singular goal of returning my grandchildren to their parents in one piece at the end of my shift.

8

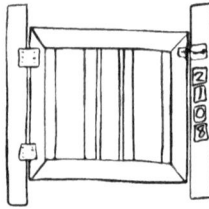

FIRST DAY ON THE JOB

My new job began in earnest four months after my hip replacement (and retirement). Jess' maternity leave was up, so Oakland called. The plan was to be Oakland two days a week, driving there on Monday mornings and returning home on Tuesday afternoons. I viewed this new job with some trepidation for a variety of reasons.

First, I am not great with babies. Second, I am not fond of driving. Getting to my destination meant driving in Bay Area traffic, which often means bumper to bumper traffic at breakneck speeds. Third, it meant getting up and on the road by 4 a.m. to ensure I was there by 6, when Jess' work day began. I really had no problem getting up early – I get up at 3:30 a.m. five days a week, BUT I do so to meditate in the pool, not to get into a car and dodge aggressive drivers. Fourth, I was due to watch my granddaughter Cameryn in this 800 square foot space, 150 of which was used by Jess for work and another 300 of it was bathroom and master bedroom areas. Jess did not have the luxury of a designated room in which to work or the pleasure of a door to close. She was planted in a corner of the common living area. What were we to do and where would we do it? And lastly, again, I am not great with babies.

I was nervous that first day, which meant I did not sleep well. I tossed and turned and checked the clock every hour or so. Traffic to the East

Bay from Sacramento is unpredictable. It can flow smoothly, come to a screeching halt, or crawl along for miles without any notice of what is going on or any discernible event to explain the inconvenience. I did not want to be on the freeway when I was supposed to be changing diapers. I rolled out of bed at 3:15 instead of my usual 3:30, took a shower instead of immersing myself in a pool, and drank my coffee in record time. I was out the door and in my car at 3:50. Oakland is about 90 miles away and a pretty straight shot from Sacramento via freeway. On a good day, the trip takes one hour and twenty-five minutes. In rush hour, it can take two hours and thirty minutes. It is hard to make it under 1 hour and twenty-five minutes unless of course you leave in the middle of the night as I do.

The drive was fairly smooth until I hit Fairfield, about thirty-five minutes away. At that location the freeway opens up into five lanes. Every single lane came to a halt. I did not have a smartphone then, which was not very smart of me. I had no idea what the problem was, but I knew I would be late. Since it was my first day, I was understandably upset. I called my son Sean to deliver the bad news. I have no idea how I expected him to handle it – I think I was afraid it would ruin their day and since it was so early, that would make for a very long day. Sean tried to reassure me that it was okay. The girls were not even up yet and Jess did not really start work at 6:00 anyways (what!!!???!!!). After about twenty minutes, the traffic began to inch forward, released from the bondage caused by the unmarked road work, and I continued to my new assignment.

My destination was an apartment in the Oakland Hills. Sean and Jess had recently moved there. I did not understand nor could I appreciate what the Oakland Hills were until I saw the area for myself that first day and walked those hills all the days thereafter. I turned off Route 13 and traveled South on Mountain View Boulevard. I took a left at Snake Road. That name alone should have given me an idea of what was in store for me. Snake is a long winding road that carries its travelers up to the Hills. One mile up I knew I needed to make a right turn on Zinn. I did not know that turning onto Zinn was like climbing up a steep roller coaster – suddenly the angle of incline went from a curvy 30 degrees to a scary 70 degrees. I was sure the coffees I bought for all of us were going to spill over in the front seat of my car, leading to a melt down before my job even began. Thankfully, the coffees survived the turn. I continued up Zinn for a half mile at which time the car and I leveled out. I drove another 100 feet and then the car plummeted down Drake Drive in search of the apartment.

2108 – An address number marked the location I was looking for. I stopped my car along the side of the road, but I could not see a house. I parked, got out of my car and peeked over the wooden gate that bore the address number into a sea of darkness. As my eyes began to adjust to the surroundings, I could make out stairs. I opened the gate and walked cautiously and quietly down those steps. I walked down to one landing and then saw more stairs, which took me to the second landing. Ah ha, the house was in front of me. I turned around to see from where I came – one might call this subterranean, but the door in front of me was not the door to Sean's place. Sean told me his door did not have a window and was on the side of the house. As I looked around, a flood light snapped on, triggered by my motion. I walked to the left and looked around the corner to find another flight of stairs going even further down into the Earth. I tiptoed down those stairs to the third landing where I came upon a door without a window. I knocked uncertainly and quietly. It was only 5:35 a.m. and I did not want to disturb the sleeping baby. Sean opened the door – finally a familiar face! Behind him stood his beloved bulldog, Gronk, and behind Gronk was Sean's lovely wife Jess, uncharacteristically disheveled, with a screaming baby in hand.

9

RAINY DAYS

My son Sean was a very irritable baby – he screamed every waking moment it seemed and since he never slept, he screamed every moment of the day. I hoped my new charge, Cameryn, would not take after her father, but that first day suggested otherwise. Carrying on in her father's footsteps, Cameryn was miserable much of the time that I was with her. Getting to the apartment at 5:30 a.m. did not mean I had time to myself in the morning. Cameryn was up and often screaming. Thankfully, Jess nursed Cameryn, giving me moments of respite throughout the day.

My only answer to a screaming baby – really a screaming anything – is to put it outside. The screeching is not as painful as it is shared with nature rather than creating a cacophony of chaotic vibrations in my head. I could not very well put baby Cameryn outside by herself, so I put myself outside with her. Surprisingly and thankfully just opening the door to go outside quieted her down. I soon learned that being outside was the only answer to my prayers.

Cameryn and I spent that first winter together outside. Oakland does not get snow, but it can be rainy. Ironically that first year of retirement was the wettest winter in the 122 years that the City of Oakland has kept records. Every morning and sometimes in the afternoon, I bundled up little Cameryn, placed her in a front sack on my chest and took the trek up the stairs. Jess had a large clear dome-shaped umbrella that we used. I often placed it over the top half of my body and balanced it with my head instead of holding it. I had my hands full with Cameryn.

The stairs were really the least of our problems once we were out. The area is called the Oakland Hills, but that term does not do it justice. I often had to lean into the hill I was walking in order to get up it. It stressed my legs, my lungs, my fortitude, my mind. Cameryn, who was having trouble sleeping, seemed to have no such trouble once we were out. While I rejoiced in her napping, it would have been nice if she napped in her crib, so I could free up my arms and renew my energy.

I have a memory of a particularly bad two days with Cameryn. It may even have been our very first two days together. I arrived to screaming and the next day I left to the same. Cameryn was so completely out of her mind on this particular Tuesday morning that I took her outside to climb the hills at 4:45 a.m. As I made my descent from the windy hill we had just trudged up, the skyline of San Francisco was perfectly framed in front of me on one turn and on another turn, the skyline of Oakland shined brightly. It was beautiful and thankfully for the medicinal nature of the outdoors, it was oh so quiet.

As I left that afternoon, Sean walked me to my car and thanked me for taking care of Cameryn. I, of course, was gracious. I never let on that I thought he had the baby from hell. He stood there as if he had something else to say, shifting his weight from one foot to the other, and then blurted out, "You aren't going to ditch us are you, Mom? I hope you will come back next week." And there it was, my son feeling vulnerable, not wanting to put pressure on me, knowing this was a job they could do, but…understanding that misery loves company. I have lived that. I did come back the next week, and again and again and again.

10

STAIRS

Time has passed since that first day on the job. My granddaughter Cameryn is two years old, a funny little girl. I have made the trek to Oakland every week for almost two years now. I cannot reflect on the Oakland trips without thinking about those damn stairs.

There are 41 of them from street level to their little apartment. There are an additional 15 steps or so below the apartment that I occasionally walk. On a normal day, I take those stairs eight times a day. That is 82 stairs roundtrip, a 41-step descent and a 41-step climb for a total of 656 stairs on a good day. One day I counted 12 trips up and down those stairs and I actually think there was one other trip at the end of the day that my brain refuses to compute.

The stairs are wooden and steep. Thankfully there is a handrail, but the house is not new or well maintained. I would not bet my lunch money on the structural fitness of that handrail.

The first time I walked those stairs, I have to admit I was worried. I was four months post-hip replacement. Hip replacements can last up to 20 years depending on one's weight, lifestyle, and load bearing activities. I was sure that those stairs were going to burn out the new device. And, a huge concern was getting Cameryn up and down those stairs safely, that is, without dropping her. So far, Cameryn has survived my guidance and now walks up and down those stairs unassisted (I do try to stay in front of her on the way down and behind her on the way up), and the joint replacement seems to be withstanding the challenge. Only time will tell whether the stairs or the hip will win this one.

Why go up and down those stairs eight or more times a day? Well, it can be explained by neuroses and necessity. It takes me two and sometimes three trips just to get settled on the Monday I arrive. I always bring Jess a coffee in the morning. I subscribe to the theory that little surprises make for a better day. That is one trip down. I return to street level for my suitcase and bedding. Finally, I have a crate I bring every week, a crate reserved just for projects in and around their apartment, the third trip made before 6 a.m. on a Monday morning. Throughout the day there are many more trips.

I take out the garbage and the recyclables. Cameryn is comforted by the outside so on a bad day we go out three or four times a day, which means three to four more treks up the stairs. I need my own personal space once or twice a day, which sends me up to street level again to hide in my car. Finally, I buy us dinner on Monday nights which means another trip to pick up the food and a last trip at the end of the day to dispose of the dinner remnants. By the end of the day I feel as heavy as an elephant, hoisting myself up and down those stairs one last time.

Tuesday dawns and I march up the stairs again for early morning coffee and bagels. The Oakland Hills are beautiful, I guess, but I am always so focused on the stair in front of me that the beauty eludes me. By the time, I leave on Tuesday afternoon, I am completely done with those stairs. As I take the stairs for the last time on Tuesday, it is amazing how much more energy I have – how much lighter I feel – knowing I am done for the week.

It is ironic that my first job post-retirement has required me to tackle these stairs. As I find myself or more accurately remake myself in retirement, I am experiencing physical and emotional ups and downs. There is a connection between the stairs and my life right now, but I am too tired to put it together.

11

Crash – Bruin – Gloo, oh my!

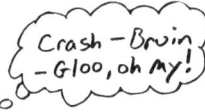

WHAT'S IN A NAME

I never thought about what life might be like with grandchildren. I did not pine for them or bother my adult children about if or when they were going to have them. I had my own thing going on. And more, I grew up in an environment where I felt a lot of pressure. I did not want to pass any of that on to my children. When the grandchildren arrived on the scene, I was happy for my children, of course, and I hoped to spend time with them as my mother's mother had with me.

My first grandson was born in 2015. His parents kept his name under cover until he was born at which time we met "Crash Odin". They actually had mentioned the name Crash prior to his debut, but we did not believe they would actually put that name on paper. They also mentioned the name Chaos, so I guess you could say we felt fortunate that they chose the former. My son-in-law, Adam, is everything rugby – player, coach, fan. He wanted to honor the sport, his son, or both by incorporating rugby into his son's name. "Crash" is a term for a rugby play. When crash ball is called, a player runs straight at the defense's line, which basically takes pressure off the backs who can then break for the outside and make a big play down field. Knowing the derivation of the name was helpful. So many people have snidely said to me, "Crash??? Well, let's hope he does not live up to his name." Yes, people are rude and now I have a retort – he is not named after a car crashing dummy, but a person crashing.

While Crash's name took us by surprise, our son and his wife chose the name Cameryn for their daughter, a very pretty name with an uncommon spelling, which she wears quite well. After Cameryn, Crash's brother arrived on the scene. His name is Bear, which we now consider quite ordinary coming on the heels of Crash. Cameryn's brother is due to arrive in November to the name of Bruin, a nod to Boston (home of the Boston Bruins) where Bruin's parents lived for four years. It seems we all have a penchant for interesting names.

I was not thrilled with the typical grandmother names so I thought my grandkids could call me "Jeannie". My name has no i and a silent e, but Jeannie was a name of endearment reserved for me by my parents on the rare occasion that they were happy with me. My daughter, the one who helped name Crash, had a different idea, of course. In high school, Kristen often called me "Mommaloo". She thought Grandmaloo would be a nice extension of that name. Grandmaloo is a mouthful for any one and the "g" alone is not an easy letter for little ones to pronounce.

When Crash began talking, he shortened it to something sounding like Goo and so I pretty much decided on "Gloo". I actually like the name – short and sweet albeit odd. Crash now calls me Gloo, Cameryn calls me "GlooGloo", and Bear surprisingly is able to sound out a hard "g". Every day I feel like I grow into my name more and more. No matter how much time I have, though, I know I can never fill the shoes of my own grandmother, Mimi, who was such a bright light in the lives of my siblings and me when we were young.

12

MIMI

My mother was an only child, born in Gaffney, South Carolina to my grandparents, Joseph and Mary McLaughlin. They were hard working throughout their lives, operating a food service for a college cafeteria to help my mom finance college, working for the federal government, writing for newspapers, and serving neighborhood kids at the soda fountain shop.

I imagine it was challenging to say the least for my mother to have eight hellions after the peace of being just one for so long. We were not model children and my mother had all she could do to just get through the day with dirty diapers and laundry. We were left to our own devices much of the time, which did not always bode well for the neighborhood or us. My father was not home a lot when I was young, working like a dog in a residency in Boston an hour away. At some point, before I came along, my mother's Mom, Mimi, decided to move closer, probably to keep us in line. She lived right up the street in a quaint white stucco ranch house, a reassuring five minutes away.

Mimi is central to my memories of childhood and the holidays, especially Christmas. She was over early in the morning preparing dinner and other good stuff, filling the house with wonderful smells. My sister Jill, fifth in line, and I slept over at Mimi's house every Friday night. Mimi would drive up to our house in her big black Ford sedan on Friday afternoons, and Jill and I would run to her with reckless abandon. That was the only time in my life that I loved riding in a car.

Jill and I watched television, made popcorn, took bubble baths and loved each other one day a week so we could be with Mimi. On Saturday mornings Mimi took us to the local doughnut shop for our favorite doughnuts. I always ordered the cinnamon doughnut and Jill had a chocolate frosted one. We sat at the shop enjoying our doughnuts, feeling loved and safe.

Mimi loved to garden: We worked out in the yard with her. Unfortunately, that experience has not helped me to tell the difference between a weed and a growing tomato plant. Mimi was a good cook and a wonderful baker. She handmade our birthday cakes, the themes determined by what we were into at the time. On my fifth birthday, my cake was topped with a merry go round of horses because I loved horses. Jill and I loved to bake with Mimi, mainly because we got to lick the sweet batter off the beaters and spoon up and enjoy the excess batter left behind in the mixing bowl.

When I was seven, Mimi suffered a debilitating stroke. Our very active and fun grandmother could no longer walk unassisted. My granddad, who had been working in Alaska, moved to Florida where the weather was kinder and took Mimi with him. We were heartbroken to lose our Mimi. We visited her once or twice a year throughout our childhood, but life changed for her and for us. I was surprised when I realized as an adult that I was just seven when she moved to Florida. She fills every corner of my being, but I only had seven years with her. That she has been such a pivotal influence throughout my life is testament to the power of love.

I could never be Mimi – hence I am called Gloo, kind of a goofy rendition of a grandmother. What she did with grace, I do awkwardly, if I attempt it at all. I am no cook but I do love to bake, although there is little creativity in what I make. Mimi's baked goods were wonderful to look at and delicious to eat. I figure one out of two is not bad: There is nothing wonderful to look at when I finish baking, but my baked goods are yummy, usually.

Glooed

I do love sharing this baking tradition with Crash, the only grandchild yet allowed to participate. As he wiggles excitedly waiting for the beaters, I can feel my sister sitting next to me as we race to spoon up the leftover batter, I hear her laughter and I see her merry little face painted with batter. Mimi cooked, baked, gardened and took us on outings. I, on the other hand, will be known for taking on the tasks that no one else notices and/or cares to do.

13

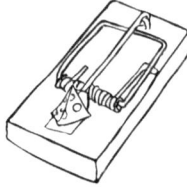

ODD JOBS

I have cleaned each of the three houses my daughter has occupied and a few apartments before she became a homeowner. The cleaning is just what I do to get rid of excess energy. My sisters call me Hazel after a television show in the early 1960's about a live-in maid for a well-to-do family. I cannot help myself, and thankfully my children and their spouses generally understand that. I used to find painting relaxing – until I helped Kristen and Adam paint much of the interior of two of their homes. I have taken on some other jobs in the name of helping my children – jobs that clearly demonstrate the depth of my own obsessive behavior.

When my daughter and her husband were first married, they lived in an older house built in the 1950's. Its exterior was covered in vinyl. Adam melted the vinyl when he used the grill too close to the house. An entire section of the back of the house sagged sadly. The backyard was quite big for a California home and had a nice pool. We spent a lot of time there and so I spent a lot of time looking at the damaged vinyl and feeling sad myself. I researched how to replace and hang new vinyl. It seemed easy enough. I needed vinyl, a special tool for ripping off old vinyl and installing new, and a special tool to cut the vinyl. I ordered the materials and watched YouTube videos while waiting for the order. The vinyl arrived in an oversized box of 12-foot sections (I had no idea) and I brought a Honda Fit, a very small car, to pick it up.

Glooed

I managed to stuff the box of vinyl into the car with the hatchback open and the front of the box resting on the dashboard and headed to Adam's house, a rather short distance away but a treacherous drive on this particular day. I had to hold down the box of vinyl with one hand and drive with the other. I did not dare take the freeway for fear that the box would slide out of the back of the car and be crushed by tire tread.

On the way to Adam's house, I stopped more than once to pull the box back up on the dash as it slipped quietly and persistently out the back. When I arrived at my destination, I took out the box (arms aching and neck twitching from awkwardly holding onto that box for dear life) and opened it up to find that the color was a good match BUT the style of the vinyl was not.

I bought the wrong vinyl and this was a custom order! I am not beyond installing two different styles of anything, but this vinyl refused to attach to the existing vinyl — and so I had to put in another order. I ultimately ordered the correct style and color and transported the second batch in a truck. The vinyl was again in twelve-foot sections and packaged in an oversized cardboard box. I leaned the front of the box up against the back of the cab so the back of the box could fit in the bed. Anyone who has ever flown a kite can imagine what happened when I was able to get some decent speed. The lightweight but awkward box flew out of the truck and landed behind the truck in the middle of the street. Thankfully, it was an early Sunday morning and the street was not busy. I sheepishly pulled over and ran back to collect the damaged box. Fortunately for me, the vinyl was not damaged. I realized then that a better way to transport this flexible material was to just take it out of the oversized box and bend it until it fit within the bed of the truck.

The installation was not any easier than selecting the vinyl had been. I learned to appreciate the phrase "measure twice, cut once" as I blew through several 12-foot sections with improper measurement technique. Again, if I could have made it fit, I would have. Thankfully I purchased more than I needed and ultimately did get the vinyl hung with little to spare.

My fingers were cut, my back ached, and my face was sunburned from two days of working outside in the hot Sacramento summer. I am sure I added a wrinkle or two to my already weathered – or is it withered – face. That was quite an accomplishment for me, installing vinyl, and I was so much happier for my daughter, knowing that the exterior of her house was uniform – which, as it turns out, she did not even notice until I brought it to her attention.

My son has avoided much of my neurotic behavior since going away to college simply because he has not lived close enough for me to obsess over his place or his family. That all changed four years ago when he moved to Oakland. He still escaped much of the pain of my neuroses until I retired, became Gloo, and was at their apartment two days a week every week. I brought my cleaning penchant to Oakland every Monday.

Sean and Jess have a beautiful English bulldog named after Gronkowski of the New England Patriots. Gronk is king of the place: He sleeps on the bed, the window perch, the couch, the floor, and drops hair wherever he goes. I figured there would be enough to keep me busy in the cleaning department if I was lucky enough to get Cameryn to nap.

A week into my job, which happened to be a week after they moved into this apartment at 2108 Drake Drive, Sean texted me a picture of an uncooked potato that had been half eaten. He informed me that it was on the kitchen counter and asked me (already knowing) what creature may have done that. I looked at the picture again, enlarged it, and could clearly see that the potato had been neatly gnawed – of course it had to be a rodent. By the time I had texted Sean back, he had investigated further, found droppings under the stove, and was off to Home Depot to get stuff to manage the problem.

Sean's place was originally an in-law apartment that was renovated to make a stand-alone apartment, presumably to generate income to help pay the mortgage. Oakland rents are so prohibitively high that a small unit can actually pay the mortgage of an entire house. The house sits at the top of a canyon and has three levels. The bottom level is essentially the ground that the house is built on. It is accessed through an old wooden hinged door on the canyon side of the house. When opened, one can see that the area runs the length of the house. From the door, the ground runs up at a 45-degree incline until it meets the far side of the floor of Sean's apartment. In other words, the house is built into the side of the hill and the bottom level is anything but level. The height of that space varies from three to eight feet. Sean's apartment is 15 steps up from the ground floor and to the left. Inside the apartment and beyond the kitchen is a door to the right that opens up into an extension of the dirt space below. The furnace is located in there as well. The space runs the length of Sean's apartment, three to four feet high and it is about ten feet wide in places giving persevering creatures backdoor access to the kitchen area.

The house is a rodent's dream – so much dry and protected area to run and roam freely, creviced and dark corners to raise families, a lot of insulation for nesting materials, and the heat from the furnace to keep them warm on cold rainy nights. Clearly these rodents had been there for some time. Sean blocked off holes in the "rat closet" that he suspected gave them access to his apartment. He told the owner who lived upstairs and assumed action would be taken.

As Sean and Jess have discovered, the owner is reactive, not proactive. The exterior of the house is plagued with dry rot and there are various entry points of which rodents can take advantage. I have since learned a lot about rodents – aka rats. They are a common problem in the Oakland Hills. Most owners hire a pest company or a handyman to manage the problem. The nexus between people and nature in the Oakland Hills is just way too close for my comfort. This landlord did not have a pest company. He also seemed to be extremely ignorant when it came to rats. He did not seem to have any idea that they carry filth and disease and breed like crazy. And so, he did nothing to address the problem. I therefore took on the job. This is where the neuroses thing seems to have gotten out of hand.

I ordered bait blocks, bought spring loaded traps, researched the best bait for those traps and the best places to lay the traps. I did not stop there. I plugged cracks and crevices with steel wool and sprayed foam insulation to close the large gaps between the walls and flooring in the rat closet and behind the kitchen area.

Every Monday, when Cameryn is napping, I get up my nerve to walk the rat closet and the basement areas. I dawn my rat gear – respirator, gloves, long sleeve shirt, long pants and shoes designated only for the rat areas – and then I check the traps and the bait blocks. Sometimes the blocks are nibbled on, a good sign and a bad sign. It means they are ingesting poison and it also means they are there.

Checking the traps is the worst – I hold my breath when I turn a corner, looking for the perfectly placed traps and I am so relieved when I find them empty. The first time I caught a rat in a trap was heart stopping. I turned the corner in the rat closet and saw the rat trap turned upside down on the ground, about two feet from where I placed it. Oh darn I thought – how did it get dislodged. As I bent down to pick it up, I saw a tail – a tail!!!! I turned around and ran back to the closet door.

Oh my God, my heart was beating so fast. I dropped my rat closet shoes at the door and sprung out of there, through the apartment and out onto the stairs. I needed to calm down – I did not want to tell Jess and I did NOT want to go back in there and pick it up. After a few moments, I gathered myself, went back into the rat closet with my phone, put on my rat shoes and walked back around where the rat trap was and snapped a picture. I sent the picture to my son and told him to send it to the landlord. Sean wrote back telling me he could not see the rat. I responded, "Look for the tail!"

My son sent a text to his landlord with the picture as evidence that yes indeed there are rats. The landlord was moved to action and called a pest company, which sent a young guy, maybe 19 or 20, out almost immediately. I had yet to get up the courage to go back in there and dispose of the thing and so I asked (begged) him to do so.

He had no problem with that request. He walked into the rat closet without a mask or gloves and took the rat trap (and rat) out in an open box. Once the rat was clear of the apartment, I tried to educate the pest guy about the dirty business of rats – and particularly, about the need to wear protective clothing and to bag the dead rat before removing it.

I suspect my advice fell on deaf ears, but I learned my lesson. Never again would I leave rodent removal to the supposed experts. I had researched the proper way to dispose of the kill and it was my goal to keep the apartment sanitary and my charges safe.

The pest guy set traps, but no time was scheduled for a return visit to check them. This was definitely a low budget operation – surprise, surprise.

A friend of mine suggested that Sean hire a pest company and deduct the cost from the rent. She simply could not understand why I would pursue such an activity. Her idea was a reasonable one and well within the law, but I didn't even consider it. For one thing, these companies are not that great at what they do. But there is something deeper lurking here that I have had to contemplate: why is it I choose to take on this dirty job? That question brought me back to my childhood of course, as that is where I look to explain my inexplicable behavior.

When I was about six or seven, my parents bought a summer house on a lake. The house was little more than a shack with running water. It had one bathroom (for the then seven kids and two adults) and three bedrooms, one for my parents, one for the oldest brother – it pays to be the oldest especially if the oldest is a boy – and the other for the rest of us. I slept on the bottom of a bunk bed.

Throughout the night I would hear scratching in the walls. At some point, I learned that rodents were in the walls – mice, my father called them. I now know that people generally say they have mice because it sounds better than rats, which is what they usually have. Learning what was in those walls was unsettling for me. I had trouble sleeping because as I would drift off to sleep, the scratching would start. That is when I discovered late night talk radio.

I would listen to the radio all hours of the night just to deaden the scratching sound. I do not know if my father ever did anything about those things. All I know is I was petrified every single night that they were going to break through that wall and land on me at any moment.

This memory, which I had buried in the dark recesses of my mind, sheds some light on my drive to exterminate. Clearly, I want to finally, once and for all, put the rodent demons behind me. And so, I bait the traps, set and place them, and take care of rat removal. I always take a picture of the catch and send it to my son.

During the time I have been watching Cameryn, my son and his lovely wife have had to deal with me on full blast. My son has no interest in taking this task on and why should he with a crazy mother like me around. Sean thanks me for my efforts, but not the pictures, and Jess tries to ignore my activities altogether. No wonder they are considering a move to the East Coast when his residency concludes.

14

GREAT EXPECTATIONS

My father's parents did not go to college, but they worked hard and succeeded at a time when a college education was not quite so commonplace or important. My grandfather was the Chief of Police in our town. He was kind to us, his grandkids, but it was clear he did not mess around. The fruits of his work ethic allowed my father to attend college. Two years in, my father enlisted in the Army and served as a medic in Europe during World War II. After the war, he attended medical school on the GI bill.

My father had big plans for his children. He expected us to attend college at a minimum and hoped some would go on to medical school. He had high hopes for me because I did well in school and I enjoyed the sciences. I did not become a doctor, but I did work hard and expected to make something of myself – presumably because I was told I could and should.

I tackled motherhood in the same way I approached my career. I read books and tried to educate myself on what was best for my children. I monitored television time and required them to do their own school projects rather than watching me do them. I taught them to clean and do their own laundry, and I expected them to help with the housework. When they were teens, I spent hours in the closets adjacent to their rooms, listening into their conversations so I could head off any troubling situations – like a party when the parents were away.

As my father had great expectations for me, I have come to discover that my children have great expectations of me. I am supposed to show up on time, in a cheery moody, and follow the parental guidelines to the tee. I have been chastised for feeding the kids too much, for breaking their meal schedule, for letting them have their way, for not letting them have their way, for letting them nap too long or not enough, for making them cookies and other yummy stuff, and for sighing (yes – sighing).

Try as I might, I often fail to meet the expectation. Sometimes the grandkids tell on me, just happy to share their experience. Sometimes I am caught on camera. Like most millennials, my children have cameras in the kids' bedrooms. I have been caught on camera failing to meet parental orders and almost immediately have been informed of the same by text. Big Brother is not the only one watching.

My children are very capable. They know how to clean and they could watch a YouTube video and learn how to install vinyl and set a rat trap, if they cared to. My obsessions are not theirs. I suspect I exhaust them. I exhaust myself, honestly. Unfortunately, I can only blame myself for always offering, always doing, never declining, never seeing or setting boundaries. It must have something to do with my childhood….

15

FLUID THERAPY

When I was very young, three or so, my family spent one summer at Cape Cod. My father loved the ocean, my mother must have as well. I have seen pictures of them frolicking in the waves – odd, because I don't think of them as being playful. At home, there was always work to do or kids to corral – perhaps they loved the Cape because it was a time when they could let loose and enjoy life.

I spent that summer frying on the beach. My sisters tell me I fell asleep on the beach, exposed to the hot summer sun, and was a little red miserable lobster when I awoke. It must have been an event worth remembering considering it is so clear in their minds. There was no such thing as sunscreen then and my parents were probably typical of all parents – if the kid is sleeping let her be. It is amazing that none of us fair skinned Irish kids have had to deal with skin cancer. I have carried my parents' love of the ocean (but not the sun) with me. I love the sound of the waves crashing on the beach, the feel of the ocean on my face, and the motion of the ocean carrying me into shore.

While we visited the ocean off and on, I grew up swimming in a freshwater lake. During the summer months, my siblings and I were in the water from morning until night. I have remained connected to the water as an adult. I swim four to five times a week, for an hour or so. Being in the water is calming for me – it is a non-threatening place to work out my frustrations. The swishing and the swashing of my arms, the kerplunking of my legs, the busy sounds of the city muffled by the change in medium from air to water create a peace I cannot duplicate above water. No one but me knows that when I am swimming, I am often battling life's obstacles and challenges. I just look like I am placidly gliding along in the water.

My husband did not meet my entire family until after we were married. We took a trip East for that event. Tough for a guy to come into a brood like that for the first time. My father called the in-laws out-laws and he gave each out-law a nickname. Patrick was the Cowboy. My father thought anyone who lived West of Chicago was a cowboy. Patrick was struck by one thing upon meeting all of us, something about which I had no awareness. He said he never saw so many faces exchanged in one room. It seemed we were all making facial contortions at each other in response to a comment or even a movement or just because, and we had no diagnosed medical condition to explain the phenomenon. Funny I have observed my grandchildren making faces of feigned disdain, displeasure, and disgust in response to my own facial expressions. I imagine that when I am swimming, my face is doing its own talking as well. Thankfully, I swim in darkness: My face and hence my thoughts are hidden from view much of the time.

Water is my sanity and my family's salvation. It is apparent when I don't swim. I am higher strung than normal – and bothered by everything and everyone more often. When I started in Oakland, I was somewhat worried about my swim routine and therefore my mental state because Mondays and Tuesdays had been two of my swim days. I have adjusted my swim schedule and it has worked out fine. The Oakland hills give me exercise enough that I can get out my frustrations. The only difference is my venting is probably not silent. People in the neighborhood must think I am just some crazy old homeless woman walking around mumbling to myself and making a myriad of faces. Fortunately for me, it is not an unusual sight.

I share my love of the water with my grandkids. Crash and Cameryn are wiggly giggly guppies in the water. Bear likes the water somewhat if it is on the warm side, typical of a bear. I am chief lifeguard when we are at the pool, which means I am in the water with them, giving them rides on my back and playing water games. I also try to ensure they take swimming lessons just in case they need an outlet for their frustrations, a private place to let their faces talk, or a peaceful place to wash away their worries when they get older.

16

OH TO BE PAPA

Unlike me, my husband Patrick hoped for grandkids and shared that hope with me often. I just rolled my eyes. After all, Patrick idealized almost everything about our early home life together, but especially life with little ones. He was pretty much absent during our children's baby and toddler stages. He traveled often, stayed in luxury hotels, dined out a lot, wore clean clothes, and enjoyed unbroken night time sleep. His memory of those days is much different than my own.

Of course, I appreciate the sacrifices he made to ensure we had peanut butter on the table. I do not mean to sound ungrateful because I do love peanut butter. But, the reality is when Patrick was around, it was a party, and then he left and the kids turned their anger over the boring mundane life that I led towards me. I am not sure he even believes me when I say our son was very challenging and our daughter turned demon when Sean was born.

Patrick missed Sean's weekly ear infections and the screams that signaled they were back, and he was absent for the nightly fight of putting the kids to bed. He loved every moment he saw the kids, which was in small manageable doses with me playing assistant. I, on the other hand, loved them for microseconds in a long exhausting 24-hour day. Fire them up and run out the door could have been Patrick's motto. I doubted that old age would change his approach much.

When our first grandchild was born, Patrick was hands off at first. Not surprising – a baby was little more than an alien to him. He had rarely interacted with his own. As Crash began to make sounds other than crying or squawking, Patrick began to turn his attention to him. He would hold him and love him until the crying returned at which time he would hand him over and leave the room. Crash was a beautiful grandchild to have as the first because he was so chill and pleasant – good training for the both of us.

Patrick came into his own as a grandfather when Crash rounded one and headed towards two. Again, this is not surprising. Patrick is the ultimate two-year-old. Patrick's goal with Crash and the grandchildren that have followed is to please. He works to see smiles and hear laughter, which often translates into letting the kids do what they want. At a certain point in time, kids get frustrated even when they get what they want. The crying is really unavoidable, unless you are Patrick, who seems to hightail it out of the fray at just the right moment.

Patrick loves to eat. He only seems to take a break from that pastime when he is working out or sleeping. Having Crash around so much invariably meant that Crash would be exposed to Papa's diet. At three, Crash eats nuts, goldfish, potato chips and marshmallows…. Crash's dad and mom do not appreciate the chips or the marshmallow diet, but they cannot monitor everything, especially a grown adult who is surreptitiously passing out marshmallows to a toddler. They do learn about Papa's generosity, but only when Crash proudly shows his parents the little white mound peeking out from the top of a small measuring cup lovingly prepared for him by his Papa. I, on the other hand, dutifully try to follow the parental food rules. Admittedly it is easier for me as I do not have the same appetite for food. Crash clearly prefers to go to Papa when he comes over because he is the treat maestro.

Patrick is just as uncomfortable saying no to Crash as he used to be hearing him cry. After a few minutes in the bath, Crash likes to splash it up. In my world, that is when he ceases and desists or gets out. When Patrick bathes him, I can hear Patrick explaining to Crash that the water is getting on the floor, that he should not splash about, that he should keep the water in the tub, asking if he wants to get out – all the while, the water continues to flow from the spigot and I imagine the water overflowing at any given moment.

Invariably someone has to come to Papa's rescue, not because Papa asks for help, but because he doesn't. Crash's laughter and sloshy water noises are deafening and concerning. When I go into the bathroom to relieve Papa, I find him on the floor next to the tub, clothes covered in water, with an exhausted and resigned look on his face. Crash smiles demonically and seeing reinforcements, he readies himself to get out of the tub.

When our children were little, we were discouraged from using the word no. Child experts thought it was bad for a child's self-esteem. Rather, we were told to give them choices we could handle. I found myself turning purple trying to come up with acceptable alternative choices to plugging the toilet with toilet paper! It seems that prohibition has been lifted, which has not helped Patrick at all.

He has a new ploy lately that irks me, using my name in vain. When Crash prepares to do something that Papa does not want him to do, he merely says, "Gloo will be mad if you do that." If Crash does not clean up after himself, "Gloo does not like that. You better pick up before Gloo sees it." I am just waiting for him to say, "Gloo says no."

I am frankly annoyed as this is a lose-lose proposition. If I agree with Papa, I am the bad guy. If I disagree with Papa, I am afraid I may have more messes on my hands in the future. In either case, Papa is the good guy looking out for his grandson by protecting him from big bad me.

I have always heard how fun it is to be a grandparent. You get to do a lot of activities with the grands and you do not have the same worries that a parent has. Now that I am a grandparent, I would revise that statement. I say it is good to be a grandfather, weaving in and out of the children's lives, casting spells of laughter and fun, sprinkling them with goodies and treats, and then disappearing before their very eyes, leaving them wired and tired and in need of a stern *No*!

17

COMATOSE

When my children were little, I refused to part with them. Patrick would suggest a trip and offer his mom (Grandma) to watch them. I would decline. Grandma raised five children and they have grown up to be successful and hardworking, so I had no reason to worry about her. I knew she would cook for them, read to them, play with them and love them. I was not really concerned about Grandma; it was Grandpa that I worried about.

While Grandma was actively engaged with the grandkids, Grandpa was actively engaged with the rocking chair. Inevitably, Grandma would have to leave Kristen and Sean with Grandpa and that was what worried me. Grandpa would be able to attend to them for a short period of time, as long as he had not popped a beer, but he would not be good for the long run. It is not that he would be completely absent. But, he seemed to be blind and deaf to things that would scream out at a normal person.

When Sean was three and Kristen was five, I relented on a suggested trip. I still do not know how Patrick pulled that one off, but he booked a trip to Marco Island in Florida. Marco Island was clear across the country offering no way of getting back easily if I got on that plane, which I did. We went with Patrick's brother and wife. That trip was difficult for reasons beyond my worry over the kids, but suffice it to say

I was glad to get back. My children were glad to have me back too. I learned from Sean and Kristen that Grandma may cook more than me, but sadly for them, my food was more palatable. Who wouldn't prefer pizza, cereal, and boxed macaroni and cheese to real home cooking of sloppy joes and porcupines? (Don't know what a porcupine is? I didn't either until I met one. A porcupine is a half of a green pepper stripped of its innards, stuffed with rice and ground beef and then baked. It may have helped if Grandma cooked the rice).

Dinner time became a war zone if the kids refused Grandma's food. Sean was a picky eater – ate cereal morning, noon, and night. Grandma was sure she could break him of that habit while I was gone, one way or another. Sean sat and sat at the dinner table, alternating between crying, gagging, and dozing off until he came up with the novel idea of throwing his food away little by little when Grandma was out of the room. It still made for a long dinner, but thankfully Sean was only three and had no homework to do. Kristen seemed to fly under the radar during these evening battles. She was a better eater and made less noise than her brother.

When I returned, I sized up the physical damage. The house was not as clean as I had left it. Since Grandpa was a snacker and often missed his mouth, I had expected that. I was not expecting the scratches that stretched across the sliding glass back door. Sean had helped Grandma with cleaning and he washed the door window. He must have used a rock, but I will never know. Grandma apparently never noticed it, probably because she was attending to Grandpa Kid, and Sean could not say. Grandma and Grandpa were clearly a contrast in styles – one that I see today with Papa and me, and one that now gives me a different perspective on Grandpa (may he rest in peace).

Papa was chief playmate with our children while I thought it was important to instill discipline. I had them on a schedule from the time they were very little. They had responsibilities and were required to fulfill them. My approach with the grandkids is somewhat different. I do not feel the same pressures as Gloo, but I do try to follow the parental guidelines and I use common sense when I am with the kids. While I love to bake, Cameryn is not free to eat sweets yet, so I do not bake with her. I won't give Crash any type of sweets after 3:00 in the afternoon. I remember the hell of a wired child at 8:00 in the evening and I do not want to be responsible for that. And with Bear, I do not plop him down in front of the delicious tiny legos and walk away.

Papa on the other hand seems to abide by no rules at all. He is forever asking Crash if he wants cookies or marshmallows, even though he has just been told not to offer them. He merrily throws Cameryn on a snow pile without considering that the pile might be sheer ice. He tosses Bear up in the air right after he has eaten and hands him off before the stomach contents spill out. It is amazing that the kids have survived as long as they have.

I am hyper vigilant. When I see something that needs to be done, I do it. I try to anticipate what might happen when I have the grandkids and I work to guard against it. Papa on the other hand is free-wheeling. There is no forethought or afterthought, no planning and no concern if things go wrong. Sometimes Papa just does not exercise any observation powers at all.

I went to Oakland one early Monday morning and did not return until Tuesday afternoon. Kristen picks her dog Merlin up from our house on Monday mornings and keeps him until I return. (Yes – he is her dog, but he lives with me). When I returned from Oakland that Tuesday, I walked into the house and was hit by a strange smell. I brought my stuff in and entered the family room. Merlin's bed was a bit out of kilter. I bent down to straighten it and discovered a lovely pile of vomit on the bed. Ugggghhhhhh. It had been there since Monday morning. Papa did not notice it then nor did he see it Monday night after work even though he sat in that room throughout the night watching tv and presumably snacking.

Papa and I are different sides of the coin. With one you get attentiveness to the nth degree, with the other you get a happy go lucky short-term approach. The grandkids seem to know to whom to go depending on their needs. Interestingly, Papa complains that he does not see the grands when I am in Oakland. Kristen does not bring them over. Hmmmmm, could it be that Kristen is not sure how long or even if Papa will be in the mood to attend to the kids? Sounds like a concern I had with Grandpa when my children were little. And the circle of life goes on.

18

THE GOOD IN OLD

One thing older people sometimes complain about is the way others perceive them. At 63, I am on the other side of life. My hair is gray, okay white, my skin is weathered, a nice way of saying wrinkled, and my joints are worn. Old people should be valued by our society because we do have so much to offer – in addition to babysitting, cleaning, walking the dog, taking out the garbage. But we are often cast out from the mainstream, thought to be too old to drive properly, think deeply, move fluidly.

There is a vast resource of people who have been through life and have considered the essential question of what buys happiness or more importantly, what does not, that is being wasted. I think about teachers – we are in the midst of a teacher shortage for several reasons. It is a tough job for one, it does not pay as well as other jobs, it is not glamorous, and it can be isolating.

On the other hand, it is rewarding if you like kids and can get through the tough initiation period. The problem with teaching is it takes years to develop the strategies and the presence to fend off the constant barrage of abuse that kids give us – and to cajole and engage them into learning. So many teachers leave the profession within five years due to lack of support and sheer mental stress.

School districts offer half-hearted training by actively employed teachers, who are burned out. They assign coaches who are full-time teachers and burned out. Inevitably, the novice teacher is left to his/her own devices. Why not tap into the fertile land of retired teachers? The school districts know what kind of a teacher the retiree was. There is a track record. The retirees would appreciate the work and the new teacher would appreciate the support. It seems so easy, but change comes slowly if at all.

The societal negativity towards old people really stems from an overuse of the word old. My grandson Crash and I were having a snack one day and I offered him goldfish. I snagged one of them as I gave him a cup full and popped it into my mouth. I realized it was stale and started to take his away. He became upset thinking I was denying him like I often do. I explained to him that the goldfish were "old" and did not taste good. Since that day, Crash has used the word appropriately to describe other food items that do not taste quite right or do not look good. He has told his Mama that "I want new ones. These are old."

Crash learned the term "new" moons ago. When he broke a toy truck, I told him I would have to get him a new one, which I did. "New" turned out to be a good thing – a positive thing – unlike the term used to describe me.

The term "old" rolls off my tongue too easily for my own good. The other day Crash asked to make banana bread. I began to explain to him that we could not make bread because the bananas were not old enough. I tripped over my own words trying to come up with another word for old, finally settling on the word "ripe". I told Crash the bananas were not ripe enough yet. Pretty soon he is going to be describing me as ripe.

We go to estate sales and look at "old" furniture – scarred and marked up. We go into old houses and say they smell funny. Rotting food is old and smells. By extension, old people smell. I reach for the perfume.

I have had dogs my entire life. They are members of the family and it is always so hard to let them go. My children have dogs as well. A year ago, my daughter and her husband had to part with their eleven-year old yellow lab, Patton. Patton was a beautiful boy. He was in a car accident five years prior and lost his hind leg, but he did not ever seem to know he only had three legs. Crash and I were talking about Patton recently. He asked me where he was. I started to explain to Crash that Patton was old when I realized I might be sealing my own fate. I could not say he was old and so we put him to sleep, or that he was old and he had to go away or that he was old and died. I suddenly realized there was nothing I could say that would help my own cause as an old person.

I now appreciate the need to be judicious in how I describe myself – and other old people and old food for that matter. If we want to be valued, it is always good to demonstrate value, but perhaps our choice of words could help create a friendlier culture for old people. Instead of calling things that do not taste or look right old, maybe we could just say they do not taste or look right. Instead of referring to people as old, maybe we can refer to them as the wise ones. I now understand why we use the term senior, but why did it take me until I am a senior to appreciate that. Who knows? Maybe I would value myself more if I thought of myself as wise instead of old or if I thought of myself as sharing my knowledge instead of being put out to pasture. A culture shift needs to happen now before someone comes up with the bright idea of putting me down.

19

PAYBACK

When I was young, we went to church as a family every Sunday morning. Getting us out of the house and to church on time was my father's job. It was sheer chaos. Some of us refused to leave our warm beds, stretching the meaning of "five more minutes" to dangerous and impossible levels. Some of us emerged from our bedrooms disheveled and wrinkled, as if we had slept in our Sunday clothes the night before. Some of us were belligerent, taking a swipe at anyone who came near. Some of us were patiently sweet, sitting quietly in the kitchen in our Sunday best waiting for the word to move out.

The one constant in all of this was our father's voice that rose above the din, getting louder and louder and more and more anxious as time ticked on. My father was a punctual man. We always attended the 8:00 Mass which meant we were there and seated no later than 7:55. The only way to ensure timeliness in that mess was to get us started early and then keep on us until we were in the car.

I was often the first one out the door because I was like my father – anxious and high strung. I was an early riser and had no use for "getting ready". Throw on the obligatory dress and slip into some comfy shoes and I was ready – after brushing my teeth that is. I may not have always brushed my hair.

The last one out the door was always my mother. As we all sat in the car waiting, my father would bellow, "Goddamnit where is your mother!" My mother would ultimately emerge, beautifully put together. As beautiful and as stylish as she was, her face was always set in a frown as she got into the car, knowing full well the wrath of my father. We would then go to church, line up in order of birth year and walk down the aisle single file with my mother somewhere in the kid mix and my father bringing up the rear. We dutifully said the prayers, reluctantly sang the songs, winced as my mother joyfully prayed and sang to God, and wiggled our way through the seemingly endless mass. At least one of us would get a swift foot or an ice-cold look from my father, punishment for too much wiggling and giggling.

This was a routine that went on every Sunday until I was in high school. The seemingly devout and devoted Irish Catholic family dressed in their Sunday best entered church every week in an orderly single line and knelt as expected during the mass. We were not allowed to do a half kneel (with butt perched on the bench) without risking a good old-fashioned kick in the behind. The only exception to the all in on Sunday occurred when my mother was too pregnant or had a baby that was only days old. She would stay home on such occasions. In retrospect, I suspect that those times were probably the most peaceful mornings she ever experienced. Kids were out of the house – no toe tapping, hand clapping, body slamming, and no husband berating. No wonder she had baby after baby.

I was not an easy child, but I was also fourth of eight. What child wouldn't be difficult? There was clearly no time for me and I had inherited my father's quick temper and impatient nature. My childhood frustration is frozen in time in family pictures – one picture in particular comes to mind.

I was dressed in my Easter best along with my two older sisters, Deb and Colleen and my mom. My mother was maybe five feet two inches tall on a good day, but in this picture, she seemed so much taller. I was then about three, Deb five and Colleen six. All of us were beautifully dressed. We were all holding hands. Deb, Colleen, and my mom wore pretty smiles while I stood off balance between my mom and Deb, shoulders hunched, eyes squeezed tight, cheeks puffed out as if I was holding my breath apparently trying to unleash myself from the grip of my mother and sister. That picture was clearly a foreboding of things to come. While I wore and bore the foibles of my father, he was away so much he did not have to deal with himself in me until I was quite a bit older. My poor mother was not so lucky.

My daughter Kristen was born a chill girl. I remember laying eyes on her for the first time. She lay on my chest, gripping my finger and looking at me peacefully and placidly. Kristen slept a lot her first year. She was her father's girl for sure. They enjoyed each other's company on weekends. Patrick lay on the couch watching sports with Kristen nestled comfortably on his chest sleeping. We have so many pictures of Kristen as a baby sleeping, on the floor, on her dad, in the car, in my arms. Over time, Kristen proved to have her father's mostly patient disposition and perhaps some of my mother in her too. She was and is stylish, particular about how she looks, and beautiful. She does not like to be rushed, it flusters her. Sadly, I flustered her often when she was in elementary school.

Kristen loved to sleep and she loved breakfast as well. Those two loves were often in conflict during the week – or in conflict with me – simply because she always was pushing the time envelope in getting out of bed and then she had to eat before going to school. Kristen loves food – and did as a child too, another thing she took after her father. She relished her time at the kitchen table and she took her sweet time. I am surprised I have any hair left. Ultimately, Kristen's slowness and my anxiety came head to head and I had to employ extreme measures. I warned her that if she could not get up and ready in a timely way, I would put her in the car in her pajamas. I do think I had to pick her up once and carry her to the car in her night clothes. I do not believe she actually walked into school that way. I think that strategy helped to get her moving a tad bit faster. I do feel bad all these years later that I created a rushed and chaotic experience for my own children, but I blame it on my father.

My son on the other hand is my father in me. He was born screaming and kicking and spent his first year doing just that until he could get on his own two feet. He did not enjoy napping on Patrick's warm body at any time of the day – he did not enjoy sleeping period. Before he could walk, he would grab onto my leg to keep up with me while I walked around the house cleaning, which I did often. Inexplicably, he could not get enough of me even when I was in the same room. Loving me was hard on him and harder on me.

Sean's birth marked the end of a peaceful existence for my husband, daughter and me. He was a frustrated boy until he could truly communicate and get around independently. To quell my own rising frustration over my out of control boy, I would lock myself in the bedroom and do pushups. I did more pushups in his first year than at any other time of my life.

Sean was and is punctual as well. When the kids were in elementary school, Sean and I would sit in the car waiting for Kristen to stumble out of the house in the morning. There is nothing worse than two anxious people feeding off each other in a confined space. He would get as crazy as me because he did not want to be late. I would honk the horn and then honk it again. That is not really a healthy way of getting the attention of a slow poke. Yes, Kristen ultimately came out, but she was so frustrated and unhappy that having her get out in time did not feel like success.

I have always said if Sean had been our first born, we may never have had a second. Kristen lulled us into thinking that babies were easy, and so we elected to have another. Whew, what a ride it was! Having to see myself every day outside the confines of a mirror was humbling and instructive all at the same time. Sean was my payback for the sins of my childhood.

My children survived me as I survived my father. They are adults now with their own children. They do a much better job of parenting than I did. They are more patient and they have strong partners who are there day in and day out to parent with them. I do not know if they see themselves in their children, but I have to say I sure do.

Crash is a thoughtful sweet soul. He likes to take his time when he does stuff, whether it be eating, playing or going to bed. He has both his dad and his mom's personality. I can see that his failure to respond to Mom is exasperating for her – she calls once, twice, three times and still sometimes there is no response. He is so focused on whatever he is doing that he just cannot break away. Kristen was the same way. Talking to her when she was doing something was an exercise in futility.

I can handle Crash's meandering way as Gloo much better than I could handle my daughter when she was young. Of course, the big difference is time, I have time to sit and wait. I do not have to hurry Crash or put him in the car dressed in his pajamas because I have nowhere that I need to be. It is very liberating for me, but on the rare occasion that I am trying to get Crash to go home after a few hours of watching him, the old feelings of anxiety and frustration percolate.

Crash also has a sizeable part of his father in him. Like his dad, Crash is interested in how things work and comes up with creative solutions to obstacles in his path. Adam is uncomfortable with any kind of attention and says he was embarrassed even as a child watching his brother perform in theater. Being embarrassed would not seem to be a genetic trait except that Crash appears to suffer the same malady. Crash becomes uncomfortable with what he considers to be undue attention. If we greet him too exuberantly, we send him into a tailspin.

Bear has shades of the bad seed in him when he is hungry. His scream can be ear piercing. We cannot put the food on his table fast enough. Absent meal time, Bear is a happy little boy. He seems to have his father's disposition, mellow, independent, and persevering. I suspect he will gain more and more self-control as soon as he is able to get his own food.

Granddaughter Cameryn, if she didn't occasionally wear her mom's reserved and knowing facial expression, I would think she was spun from Sean's genetic material only. Cameryn was born screaming and she kept it up for five or six months. Sean and Jess will say she was pretty easy the first month or two. I cannot attest to that, but if so, she was just storing up steam for the months to come. At two, Cameryn still flaunts the impatience of Sean. If she cannot get her baby to fit just so in the stroller, she cries out with frustration. She refuses any help going up the 41 steps from their apartment to the street and bats away a helping hand. Cameryn gives the guy who blessed her with this dimension of her personality a run for his money. They often mirror each other's actions and reactions, which is pretty funny when you think that one of them is two and the other is nearing 32. The blessing of the mirroring is Sean has a great laugh and Cameryn does too.

I do not think I ever warned my children that their kids would be payback for their own sins. That was a sentiment I heard often when I was young. Had I said it, they would not have believed it. Living with their "mini-me's" every day gives them a dose of their childhood transgressions and provides me with some free entertainment.

20

I DO

At 63 years old, I am still surprised by the roles I have taken on – wife, mother, grandmother. This was not in my plan at all – in truth I had no plan. I did not know what I wanted out of life; I only knew what I did not want. I did not want to marry, having no good example to coax me. My father was authoritarian for sure – the man of the house literally and figuratively. My mother had all she could do looking after eight children. At some point in her life, long before I came along, she was a strong and self-sufficient soul. She served as a cartographer for the U.S. Army Map Services in Washington, D.C., during World War II, doing top secret work identifying enemy locations in Europe. After the war, she met and married my father, became a mother and a wife, and lost herself.

I did not want to be my mother – I did not want to be controlled by anyone, but certainly not by a man called husband. The only surefire way to avoid that in my mind was to say no to marriage.

In keeping with my philosophy to remain free and true to myself, I never dated much – a guy in college until he decided to dump me for a roommate and a date in high school arranged by my mother – yes, sad. I never felt like I was missing out, except around prom time. I did not go to junior or senior prom. I have been to a lot of weddings since though and I imagine a prom is kind of like a wedding, but weddings (as long as they are not your own) are a lot more fun.

I moved away from home within a week of college graduation. My parents gave me $500 as a graduation gift, which I immediately applied to a plane ticket, destination Salt Lake City Utah, 2500 miles from home. I had a friend in the military who was stationed there. Utah was the furthest place I could go and have a place to stay. I had not planned on a one-way trip. It was my intention to visit for three or four weeks and then return to Massachusetts.

But, my friend worked every day. I became bored and decided to check out the job scene. I found a lab job fairly easily, starting a new chapter in my young life. I never looked back. That is not to say I did not miss my big sprawling family. I missed them terribly, but I guess I was taken by the beauty of the mountains and the peace of my new life. I spent good money over the years going back to visit and ensuring my children knew their grandparents, aunties, uncles, and cousins, but I never considered moving back home.

I met my husband about a year after I moved to Utah. I landed a job at the University of Utah in a toxicology lab and he worked at the same lab part time while attending the university. At first sight, I was not impressed – just another arrogant guy. He paid no attention to me either. He was apparently equally unimpressed. As time went on, I did become interested in Patrick. He loosened up – or I did – or we both did. We were together a lot since the lab space was small. And then there was a party and people from the lab were invited. I am surprised I even went – I was still something of a loner – but I did go and that is when we became a couple. I later learned that Patrick had commitment issues too. He had a rule to discard after the expiration date of three or four months. I guess I grew on him because he was unable to shake me after those first few months, although he did try. By then I was enjoying him – he was a welcome break to the quiet of my then life.

About six months into our relationship, we moved into an apartment together. In those days, living together in an unmarried state was not widely accepted. I really did not see the writing on the wall. Living together was a far cry from being married. I had no trepidation about living together because I had no expectation beyond that. A few months into our cohabitation, Patrick changed the dynamic by asking me to marry him. I did not say yes immediately. In fact, I struggled with that question. I did not want to hurt him by saying no, but I did not want to hurt myself by saying yes. I ultimately did say yes, which made my mother very happy. She had been sending me two dollars with every letter to purchase a marriage license. She was afraid I was going to Hell for living in sin.

I said yes, but I wanted to rescind my answer many times in the days before we married. We planned our own wedding, which proved to be an embarrassment to my parents, but just our style. It was a low maintenance, low budget deal – maybe $500 including the $23 dress I bought from J.C. Penny for the occasion. We probably had 20 people at our wedding, no flowers, no pomp and circumstance. We invited another 15 people to our reception, half of whom were on Patrick's rugby team. The reception consisted of a kegger in the backyard of Patrick's parents' house with music provided by his brother's stereo.

Two days before the wedding my parents flew in to Salt Lake with my four younger siblings. The night they arrived, I went to dinner with them and Patrick stayed behind. My father produced a one-way ticket home for me. He told me he knew I was only getting married because I was lonely and so invited me to return to Massachusetts and rejoin the family mess. That was the nail in the coffin for me, the only thing more preferable than going back home was staying where I was and getting married. Two days later my father walked me down the seemingly infinitely long aisle of the church in my J.C. Penny dress and blue flip flops and I said, "I do."

I soon realized that saying I do was only the beginning of being married and my reluctance was well founded. Patrick planned a "honeymoon" for us in Seattle. We drove to Seattle with Patrick's parents (yes, his parents). They lived in Sekiu, Washington and Seattle was on the way. You could say they were giving us a ride, so I should have been grateful.

We stayed in a motel (we did have our own room) and had a honeymoon dinner at the Space Needle, just the two of us. The next day, Patrick and his parents dropped me off at the airport to return to Salt Lake, and Patrick continued our honeymoon with his parents. Patrick loved his mother more than me, apparently, and he was a college student on summer break who needed a respite from his newly married life. I was working full time and I had no more vacation days. Thankfully, work called giving me an excuse to cut short my honeymoon with his parents.

I seriously debated changing the destination of my ticket to Boston at that point. Getting married was looking like a big mistake. Fortunately or unfortunately for me, returning to Massachusetts, especially in a defeated state, was not a palatable option. And so, I returned to Salt Lake bearing an invisible married stamp on my forehead.

My struggles with being married had a very practical and immediate effect. I signed the wedding license with my maiden name – not mindfully intentional, but intentional nonetheless. My father had clearly wiggled his way into my being. He always told his children that all you really have in life is your name. At 24 years old, I could not imagine giving up my name for the name of someone I knew for only a year. There were some raised eyebrows and maybe hurt feelings on my husband's side of the family, but they really had no room to complain. After all, I did allow them to join us on the honeymoon!

Even though we lived in sin for some time before getting married, the power struggles of life together did not truly begin until after we tied the knot. We silently tussled over where the silverware should go – literally, in which slot the spoons and the soup spoons should rest – and who would get to the sink of dirty dishes first. I believe we went three weeks once before those dishes were washed (although I am sure that is my exaggerated mind at work) and I was the one to give in. But the real work of being married has taken decades for me, and it continues. Thinking "we" and accepting help were foreign notions. Strangely enough, becoming Gloo has helped me to be a better person all around, which means it has helped me to be a better wife as well.

21

WE

I spent my young life working on being independent. My father often made us sit through his bill paying sessions to ensure we knew how much we were costing him, particularly the money spent at the department store that the older kids frequented for clothes. Of course, he did provide them with charge cards with which to make their purchases.

My parents did not have to worry about me spending money on clothes. I had a very limited wardrobe, governed by what felt comfortable and most things did not. When I found something I could tolerate without itching or feeling confined, I wore it until the threads of the fabric unraveled or my arms grew out of the sleeves. Ironically, I often overheard my father complaining about my choice of dress. He actually wished I would spend money on clothes and look more presentable, I suppose.

I took to heart the complaints about money or the lack of it. At an early age, I decided I did not want anything from my parents, not clothes or money. I was pretty content if I did not get any attention as well. As my siblings and I grew older, my father often held us hostage by saying he would not pay for this or that if we did not follow his directives. Money was a way to control us – the worst was telling us he would not allow us to go to college. We all looked forward to college to escape the madness of our house, so that was a threat that hit home. When it was my time to go to college, I was more than ready.

My father made the usual threats. I did sometimes worry about whether or not I would be attending the next semester, but these occasions were often countered by a good grade report and a jubilant father who felt his money was well spent. I did not accept any personal spending money. The power to give came with the power to take away and my father had used the take away power enough that I did not trust the arrangement. During the school year, I lived on my summer savings and the money I earned from working in the cafeteria and cleaning up after the sloppy, spoiled college kids.

Life for me was all about being independent, about what I could do to help myself. There was another element involved as well. Not only did I want to count on myself, it was an absolute necessity because I did not feel that I could count on anyone else. My mother struggled with raising eight ruffians and dealing with an angry husband. My father worked a lot, drank a lot, and when home he bothered us a lot, and my siblings struggled to find themselves and a way out from the oppressive reign under which we lived.

The only person I had ever really counted on was my grandmother, Mimi. She was there every Friday as she said she would be, to pick up my sister and me. She took us out every Saturday. She was there for every holiday. She taught me to trust. Sadly, when she left my life, so too did that fragile thing called trust.

No wonder I had trouble being a spouse! Getting married was scary, but being married was beyond scary and oh so hard. My dear husband Patrick was patient. It seems that each day we began again at square one – the progress of the day before vanishing into thin air. Patrick stuck with me, for which I am and will always be grateful. Because of his tenacity, we had children and our children had children, who turned out to be my ultimate teachers on how to be one of two instead of just one.

Crash and Bear live right around the block from us – literally the next street over. While Crash spends half of his life at our house or coming or going from our house, he does not think of the house as Gloo and Papa's house but as Gloo's house and Papa lives in it with Gloo.

Because my daughter's family lives so close, we get visits all the time, some announced and some unannounced. In all cases, Crash will walk into the house and want to know where the missing piece is. If I answer the door, Crash needs to know where Papa is. If Papa answers the door, Crash asks where Gloo is. He is happiest when we are together.

After dinner, we often get a call from Crash inviting us to go on a walk. He doesn't call Gloo or Papa, he calls Gloo AND Papa. We generally put the phone on speaker because while I may answer the phone, he expects Papa to be right there as well. His call goes something like this. "Hello Gloo, you and Papa want to go on a walk with us?" Of course I say yes. He then says, "Papa, you want to go on a walk with us?" More often than not, Papa is within ear shot and answers for himself. On the few occasions that Papa is not around, Crash is somewhat confused because to him we are one.

Funny thing is, Cameryn, who lives 90 miles away and does not see us every day, has managed to link us together too. When we FaceTime, Cameryn sees me and says, "Papa?" and when she sees Papa she asks for "GlooGloo".

Our children have joked for a long time about the way Patrick and I dress. We seem to dress alike with no preconceived design or thought. There are several pictures of us at different events with the same colored shirt and pants. We walk around the block in our gray baggy sweats. People we don't know think we look alike and have wondered if we are siblings. Despite all of this, I had trouble mentally with bridging the gap between "me" and "we" until the grands came along. Patrick and I are their Gloo and Papa – not either one alone but two together. The grands have taught me that two is better than one – whether it be Gloo and Papa or husband and wife. Hallelujah, forty years in and I think I am shedding the me for we.

22

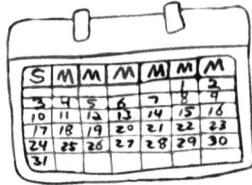

EVERY DAY IS MONDAY

Some folks have a blast in retirement. They take classes, golf, go to the beach, volunteer, enjoy coffee on the patio, and garden in the yard. They set their own schedule, do what they want when they want, and seem to be beholden to no one. These people give retirement a good name and make people not yet there yearn for the day they can retire. Those adept at retirement seemed to have a plan for what they would do and the mindset to not only implement the plan, but to reinvent themselves as well.

I missed the planning phase of retirement. Of all people, I needed that time because I am so regimented. Casual friends would see me at the gym and gush over my new state – how is retirement, aren't you just loving it? Actually, I am somewhat embarrassed to be retired. Once I healed from the hip replacement, I felt fully functional, like I should be out in the field plowing with all the other workers. I thought I was too young to be in this unemployed state, even though my face may have told a different story.

Retirement for me, and probably for many retirees, does not mean an absence of work, but a different kind of work, not as rigorously scheduled but scheduled nonetheless. Instead of teaching and guiding 13 and 14-year olds, I am being stretched and pushed by toddlers. Instead of grading papers, I am coloring, finger painting and constructing stuff with Play Doh. Instead of helping to develop the minds of 8th graders, I am sitting in toddler music class learning songs with finger play and hoping to keep my own mind going. My schedule varies with the day of the week.

On Mondays and Tuesdays, I am in Oakland with Cameryn. We have fairly full days – checking out different parks and going to the Kids' Gym in Berkley, the Little Farm in Tilden Park, the grocery store, and music classes. We are out and walking with a group of senior ladies, self-titled the neighborhood watch group, by 8:30 in the morning.

On Wednesdays, I am back in Sacramento taking Crash to music class. When the weather is nice, we go from music to Fairytale Town, enjoying snacks along the way. Crash insists on a stop at Gloo's house before going home. There is nothing special there, but he loves the routine.

On Thursdays, I take Crash to swim lessons. On Fridays, my daughter works and I take care of Bear. Saturday and Sunday come along and we are on call. Kristen usually works at least one weekend day. Papa and I try to take the kids for half of that work day to allow Adam to prepare for his week ahead.

While my week is full, I am easily frustrated since I have not quite accepted my lot. People tell me how lucky I am to have this time. What greater purpose is there than being with one's grandchildren? Yes, cleaning up stomach contents five times a day or singing Trot Old Joe for the tenth time in an hour is rewarding and who needs uninterrupted meals and bathroom breaks. I feel blessed to have the grands in my life, yes, but as a caretaker I know I am not the best.

And too, sometimes, I just want a Saturday and a Sunday to tie up loose ends, to clean my house, to watch television. Ahhh, the good old days call to me, the days when I worked full time. Back then, I could count on relaxed, kick back Friday nights, enjoying a cold beer with the weekend ahead of me. My week days were full with teaching, grading, and after school activities. I enjoyed Gloo duties occasionally, but then there was only one grand and a stay-at-home Dad. Saturday and Sunday meant time to clean, get ready for the next week, watch sports, and breathe.

Fast forward to retirement and on a typical Friday night, the house is littered with toys, and filled with the grands' screeching voices. In the midst of it all, my adult children, their spouses and Papa sit with their feet up on the table, having a drink and celebrating the beginning of their weekend. Retirement for me, what does it mean? Retirement for me means every day is Monday except for Sunday, sometimes.

23

ARM'S LENGTH

I have an intimacy problem, which I suspect began very early in life. I have a fairly early memory that highlights my young discomfort with human touch. I was less than three and in the hospital for eye surgery to correct my cross-eyed look. I am standing in a crib with patches on my eyes listening to my favorite television show *Lassie* (about a boy and his dog). At some point, those patches were removed. The first person (and only family member) I remember seeing was my grandmother, Mimi.

Mimi brought me a gift, a duck that magically bobbed by itself, seemingly taking in some water and then returning upright. I know now that it was just science in action, but at the time it was magic to me. I also received a fairly large stuffed toy Collie, just like Lassie, that shared the crib with me, making me feel happy and safe. I do not really know how long I was in the hospital, but I do remember going home. I was happy to get out of that crib, which I viewed as an indignity. After all, I was not in a crib at home – we had one crib and were booted out early in life to make room for the next baby in line.

Mimi picked me up and brought me home. I remember coming through the door of our small full house. Directly ahead upon opening the door was a stairway that went upstairs. The hallway with the big oval mirror was to the left leading straight into the kitchen. My mom was sitting on the stairs when I came in. I can distinctly remember her smiling widely with arms outstretched, calling to me. I went to her and she pulled me close and hugged me tightly. My mother was not a demonstrative person. She was quietly stoic and rarely gave out hugs, kisses and "I love yous". On this day, she held me too close and for far too long. While I understand now that she was pouring all of her worry and energy into my small body, that moment was uncomfortable enough to win a spot in my memory bank for life.

It seems my own nature for nurturing and loving was being constructed then, piece by piece. I am not a touchy-feely kind of gal. I appreciate a good distance between myself and the person next to me. As a basketball player, I was told to keep the opposing player at arm's length so I could react to his or her movements. I apply this rule in life as well to ensure others are a safe distance from me and, secondarily, to measure my appropriate proximity to others.

Crowded events are troublesome as my body inevitably comes into contact with the body of a person next to me. I hate being in a line with others as invariably someone will come up behind me and stand close enough that I can hear and sometimes feel that person breathing and even worse, occasionally smell that person's breath. Anyone who has ever been to Costco when they are doling out unhealthy treats with reckless abandon should be able to relate.

As a teacher, I never gave hugs, touched, or stood too close to my students, which I am sure they appreciated. My husband often jokes that he does not know how we ever had children since I have such a problem with proximity. Thankfully he does not have my malady – he is a nurturer and he ensured that our children had lots of hugs and kisses when they were little.

While I was not as free with the hugs as was my husband when the kids were little, I did break out of my mold when necessity called. My son had night terrors when he was little. Sean woke us up every night, tormented by demons that he could not bear and about which he could not remember in the morning. We exhausted suggested remedies, ultimately settling with him coming into our bed when he needed to, which happened to be nightly for a year or so. I can still feel his warm breath on my face as he woke me up whimpering about the night's demons. He would crawl up into our bed, and quickly fall fast and deeply asleep, tucked into the curve of my body as I held him close. Those were precious moments, I now know. But, my children have long since flown the coop and my proximity aka intimacy issues have deepened with age, as idiosyncrasies often do. And then the grands came along.

Babies are soft and huggable like stuffed animals. Even so, I never had the urge to touch, hold or hug a baby before the grands arrived. I would rather hug a stuffed animal any day. They are safer to handle, make no noise, and hold up to being crushed, dropped, or squeezed. I was nervous with Grand #1, felt like I was holding a fragile porcelain doll. The trusting soul that he was, he gave me time to adjust – he was very tolerant with me as I changed his diaper and tried to rock him to sleep. Over time, Crash grew more solid and focused, so I was less of a danger to him. He is a very active little boy now with little time for hugs and cuddles. As he gains language, Crash expresses himself easily. After an absence, he gives me a quick hug and says with a lilt in his voice, "Gloo, I love you," and then he is off to the next project.

Cameryn has had to deal with me many more hours in a single day than Crash or Bear. She is an affectionate soul, but soooo busy. Since Mom works from home, she has access to her during the day and showers her with hugs, kisses, and giggles. At times she barely tolerates me, viewing me as the wicked nanny that keeps her from her mother. She boldly flattens her eyes until they are little more than slits, aiming to flash me with her evil eyes. She does not yet realize that she is messing with the Queen of crazy eyes.

At other times, she sees me as her playmate, the one who takes her out on explorations. She will always prefer Mom, but she is an outdoorsy kid and when the door to the world opens, she cannot resist walking through it.

Cameryn's compulsory time with me has given her a certain empathy and maybe even love for me, her Gloo. She gets excited now when she knows I am coming and greets me in the morning with a big hug.

Jeanne M. Carroll

We share some rare quiet moments where Cameryn touches my hair, hangs on the back of my neck, or drapes her arm around my neck and hugs me.

At an early age, Cameryn seemed to know when I was full, from the stairs, the hills, the demands of being Gloo. On particularly challenging days, as I carried Cameryn down the stairs for what I hoped was the last time that day, Cameryn would pat my back gently with her little hand. Cameryn still sometimes pats my back when we have had a particularly busy day – a simple but generous gesture of acknowledgement.

Bear is a big soft bowling ball of activity and sound. He graces me with a beautiful warm smile and then scoots off. There is no cuddle in him yet. As a baby he would loudly nuzzle himself into the crook of my arm until he fell asleep, and now the only time he is still is when he is sleeping. Ironically, I, the one with the proximity issue, willingly come within arm's length of Bear, giving him loves and getting back giggles as I bury my face into his chest. Bear does not want to be held for too long, so these are fleeting moments.

As far as the grands are concerned, the arm's length rule simply does not apply. At some point, I know they will want their distance and I will be fine with that, but for now, I am good with the contact – the kisses, hugs, and pats on the back. How close is close enough? When it comes to my grands, close is as close as they want to be.

24

SIBLING LITTLES

Throughout our childhood, my father told my siblings and me, "Your brothers and sisters are your best friends." When you have seven siblings, they can't all be your best friends, but I have found over time that this adage has proven mostly true. Certainly no one else has known me longer or lived through the same plight of parental trial and error. And too, sometimes regular friends just don't measure up, giving siblings an unintentional leg up.

Just as I did not want to get married, I also did not want to have children. My Irish Catholic background did help with that – absent marriage, children are supposed to be a non sequitur. Even after I fell victim to the "m" word, I did not want to have kids. Growing up with siblings was fun, yes. There was never a dull moment. But, I grew up in a household where politics and world events were often discussed. Knowing what I knew about the world, I thought it was unfair to have children. The world did not deserve them. My husband ultimately won out on this score. After seven years of postponing, debating, and fretting, we had our first child. Once we were on the baby track, there was no question that we would have another. We both valued our sibling relationships enough to believe we could not leave our first born without siblings. At the same time, I knew in my heart of hearts that she would only get one.

Kristen and Sean grew up pushing and pulling, agreeing and disagreeing, separating and growing close. As kids, they sat across from each other at the breakfast table – Kristen making faces and tormenting Sean, and Sean hiding behind a wall of cereal boxes to block her out. They stood up for each other when I was hard on them and they watched each other go through heartache and heartbreak, silently consoling each other. They moved on to college and the pursuit of careers, going in opposite directions, hearts full and teary-eyed. They were each other's biggest cheerleaders and loudest critics, and then made room in their hearts and at the table for their respective spouses.

While my father touted the importance of brothers and sisters, I did not adopt the same phraseology with my own children. I hoped they would be friends for life and I tried to treat them fairly, although they did not always see it that way. Kristen always said I favored Sean and Sean said Patrick favored Kristen – well I guess that is pretty fair. It would have been a bummer if we both favored the same child. Despite this criticism, our children obviously enjoyed a good enough childhood experience that they wanted to have children, and they both thought it was important to have at least two, in fulfillment of my father's scripture.

Both families are already working with their children on the importance of siblings. Crash is not demonstrative generally, but he hugs Bear regularly and tells him he loves him. I think Crash's first uttered "I love you" went to Bear. Cameryn is big sissy to baby brother, still in utero, anxiously waiting to put him in her stroller and take him for a ride. Crash and Cameryn could be siblings. They look so much alike and they are growing up knowing each other, thanks to the collective efforts of parents and grandparents. Crash already teases Cameryn as Kristen did Sean. Hopefully they will be keepsake cousins, rather than viewing each other as the odd side of the family later in life. Brothers and sisters may be your best friends, but it doesn't hurt to have a cool cousin in your court as well.

My father sang the praises of siblings, but I don't think he gave much thought to the fact that siblings grow up, get married, and have littles, until the first grandchild called him Grampa. It must have been hard to take.

Glooed

My parents were 46 and had a three-year old when they became grandparents. My father was not ready to think of himself in that way so he chose to be called JV, taking grandfather out of the equation altogether. My mother had no preference (other than maybe not to be called at all) and ended up with the designation of Gammy, until my kids came along. I could not bring myself to call her that so Kristen and Sean called her Jellybean Gram because she always had jelly beans. My parents were nominally involved grandparents, understandable considering they suffered through every stage of childhood eight separate times. Clearly, grandparents handle this phase of life in different ways.

As for Kristen and Sean, I wouldn't say they are best friends yet. On a day to day basis, their spouses are their greatest allies. But the truth of the matter is my kids have odd parents. They lived a childhood experience that no one else can know or understand as they do. By the time they are my age, I think they are going to need each other to properly process the trauma of their shared childhood. I suspect their littles will also need each other to get through their own experience some day in the distant future.

25

DON'T LEAVE ME

As the fourth of eight, I watched three older siblings enjoy freedom before me. I watched and waited to walk, to go to school, to ride a bike, to drive a car, to go to college. While the process of watching and waiting was painful, my birth order was a benefit in the end because I saw how things were done before I had to do them and I got lost in the crowd, which was a good thing in my family. I loved school, but perhaps it was because I knew the alternative was sitting at home with kids in diapers. I loved riding bikes. It gave me the freedom to leave the house without counting on anyone else to get me places. Watching my siblings go off to college was the most painful of all. When it was my time to go, I did not look back.

My oldest started in day care at four months of age. She was not at all upset about the transition as she was so young and completely distracted by the activity around her. The only time she struggled at all was when she was three and we moved across country and plopped her into a new environment. Even still, she met that challenge in her stoic, stony-faced way.

My son on the other hand spent too much time with his crazy mother when he was a baby, poor dear. On his first day of preschool, he was frightened, enough so that I picked him up and carried him across the threshold. I was chastised by the preschool director for taking away his power. She suggested that carrying him conveyed the message that he could not meet this new challenge on his own two feet. I took that advice to heart and never again carried my children into school, church, or even a shopping center, although I may have made an exception for a fractured foot or a sleeping child. My son proved to be more than capable of motoring himself in any event, and too, he realized in short order that his sister was there to lead the way through the preschool door and childhood too.

Since they have been out of the house and on their own, I email or text Kristen and Sean every morning. There is little to no substance in my communications – just an opportunity to say hello, wish them a good day, and get a read on how they are feeling.

Some years ago I began to question the wisdom of this daily contact. I became concerned that they might be growing dependent on these communications and miss them when I am no longer here to write them. Yes, at 55 I was thinking about my passing! I stopped the daily email for a time, but the precedent had been set. My kids soon harassed me, wondering where their morning emails were. Reluctant to tell them I will not live forever, I resumed this exercise.

Despite this daily ritual, I do my best to stay out of their private lives. I do not share my personal problems, I try to be light-hearted and positive, and I keep my neurotic fears down to a dull roar. Over time I have realized that Kristen likes to have live or in person conversations while Sean prefers the terse text. I had hoped that by now they would find some comfort with each other as opposed to communicating with just me. Lately I have suggested that someday they will need to fill for each other the role I now handle. That means Kristen will need to text Sean, short and sweet, and Sean will need to set aside some time each week to talk to Kristen in person or on the phone. These are skills that neither of them presently care to have and probably will not develop as long as I am here filling that void.

Knowing that my children have partners with whom to share life is comforting and liberating as well. It means I no longer worry about what will become of them when I am not around. I love their spouses as if they were my own without having to add them to my daily email/ text responsibility. The grands, however, have stirred the worry pot anew. I find that I am always worried about something relating to the grands – their skin, calcium intake, sleep schedule, urine output, irregular head shape, the pesticides in their food, their adjustment to school….

I often take Crash to school to give his mom time to get Bear ready for the day – or herself, if she is off to work. The last few times I have taken him, Crash has become weepy even before we get to the preschool door. We had a talk about it one day and I asked him why he was sad. He said in his matter-of-fact way, "Because, Gloo, I don't want you to leave me." The very next time I took him to school, he burst out crying, reached for me as I was leaving and pleaded, "Don't leave me Gloo!" I realized our talk helped him to crystallize his thought process. Obviously, we needed to have another talk, which we had on the way home that very same day. I explained to Crash that I may leave him, but I would always come back just as I did that day. Instead of saying goodbye, we agreed to say, "See you later." Crash seemed to get it, telling me that when he is big, he will drop me off at school and we will leave each other using the same words. I told him that was a deal, thinking there may come a time when he drops me off, not at school but at Gloo daycare.

My own children never pleaded with me to stay with them. If anything, they begged me to leave. I must be a much better Gloo than I was a mom, which brings me back to thinking about my grandmother, Mimi. Mimi had two senior black Cocker Spaniels, Jeff and Cindy. Jeff and Cindy were such good dogs. They caught popcorn on the fly, patiently put up with loud rambunctious kids, sat on command and followed Mimi everywhere. I am sure my love for dogs began with them. When Mimi suffered her stroke, they were also caught in the crossfire. I never saw them after she ended up in the hospital and to this day, I do not know what happened to them. Losing Mimi and her dogs with little explanation and no preparation left me feeling sad and empty. I do not wish that on my grands and now I find myself worrying about that as well.

I worry about how they will fare in this troubled world and how they will deal with challenges and loss. Ultimately, I have to depend on their parents to manage the vicissitudes of life and the grands' responses to them. I believe the grands are in good hands or at least better off than my children were. Who am I to offer advice? And too, I know the grands will carry me with them in some shape or form long after I am gone.

When I was young, my father loaded all of us into his car on Sunday afternoons (with the exception of my mother and the most recent baby) to visit with his parents (Nana and Grampa). Nana was a large, imposing, stern woman who demanded and commanded the attention of everyone in the room. I was not a fan of Nana. My adult self believes she talked to me only when she was directing or correcting me, and she "always" washed my hair in the sink of her small, cramped bathroom, scrubbing my head raw. "Always" in a childhood memory could have been once and traumatic or weekly and traumatic. Either way that hair washing scene is etched in my mind.

The one bright spot to those visits with Nana were the rides home. Nana and Grampa lived high above the city, up at the top of a few long rolling hills and close to the local airport. On clear nights, the stars twinkled. When the moon was full, my father would point it out and tell us that the moon was smiling at us. To this day, I see a smiling benevolent face when I look at the moon. During my early morning swims under a full moon, I feel like my father is with me, commiserating over the imperfect art of parenting and laughing about my trials and tribulations as Gloo.

I suspect the grands will find something in life with which to associate me. I may be a song in their hearts, a rainbow in the sky, the smell of cookies baking, or the stairs creaking as they go up and down them. Each of the grands will figure out what it is that reminds them of me when I am no longer physically present. I just hope and pray I am not the sound of scratching in the walls.

26

NEED A BUDGET
YESTERDAY

Being retired has put a dent in the wallet. I no longer make my own money. This is a big deal for me since it has always been important for me to be financially independent. When I was working, I never spent a lot of money on my kids or myself. I believed in denying them and me: There were no shopping sprees or spontaneous purchases. My wardrobe was simple. For work, I would find the most comfortable shirts and pants (nurse scrubs became my go to) and then order four or five pair of the same style.

My casual clothes are simple and gender neutral – shorts, t-shirts, jeans, socks, and a pair of sneakers. I own two skirts that I have worn on maybe four occasions in the past ten years and two pair of dress pants that I have worn on all the other dressier occasions such as holiday dinners, weddings and funerals. My poor husband must be embarrassed to take me to workplace functions. Come to think of it, I cannot remember the last time he invited me to one.

I have no patience for any kind of shopping, clothes, food, furniture. Because of my disinterest in shopping and in what I wear, I never worried much about needing to budget in retirement.

Glooed

Two years into retirement, I find that I spend more money now than ever. I want the grands to have fun toys, kid-sized furniture and balance bikes. They grow out of their clothes so fast and since they are at my house often, I need clothes on hand. I love books and want them to love them too and so I raid the book store every chance I get.

Crash and Bear have eczema, poor dears, so I need a supply of the expensive skin cream. Buying kids' shoes is one of my things – not the cute colorful ones, but the sturdy practical kind. I have flat feet. As a kid, my mom took me to a specialized shoe store for fitting and purchase. For some reason, I suffered from ill-fitting shoes even still (or maybe shoes I had outgrown) in the form of sore feet, blisters and calluses. Somehow that experience has stayed with me. I am always checking the grands' shoe fit, anxious to buy them a new pair of shoes when the toes feel dangerously close to the end of the toe box. Their parents thank me but they are much more fashion conscious than I am. I have come to realize that they do not want their children out and about in ugly shoes. And so, I keep the shoes I buy for the grands at my house.

The advent of online shopping has only fueled my shopping frenzy. I no longer have to wade through the clothing aisles looking for what I want or deal with people that get too close. It is way too easy to just point, click, add to the shopping cart, and purchase.

I go to the grocery store far more often than I ever did. It must be strangely comical to see a 63-year-old woman push around a shopping cart filled with formula and diapers. I spend money on such recreational activities as swim, music and gym classes. These activities provide an outlet for their energy and give me the hope that they may nap well on my watch when we get home from class.

The food and recreation budget has increased exponentially in the past two years such that my husband is worried about retiring himself. He is the ultimate saver. Because of him, our kids completed college without going into debt or spending a dime of their own money. He used to have a partner that was careful about what and where she spent money, but that is no longer the case. I need to reel it in so he feels he can retire, live comfortably and most importantly, help out with these grandkids.

27

THE PROBLEM WITH GRANDKIDS

I love my grandkids. Each one of them has wiggled his/her way into my heart. They are funny, sweet, mischievous, and sassy, working on the attitude that will get them through their early teens. They are up for anything - a walk around the block, a visit to Fairytale Town, a snack, or an afternoon doing puzzles and building with blocks. They are up for anything until they are not. Even at their most stubborn, they are the sweetest, until their parents come around.

A grandparent is said to have the best of all worlds. We get to love the grandchildren and enjoy them and when they are out of sorts, we can send them home. That is not quite true in my case. I take care of Cameryn two days a week and they are solid Cameryn filled days. I am at her place. Her mom is working in the apartment 20 feet from where I am trying to keep Cameryn busy, get her dressed, whatever the case may be. We are out the majority of the day, but peeling Cameryn away from her mom and getting out the door are challenges that sometimes sap me of the little patience and energy I have.

Cameryn is a momma's girl for sure and at two, she makes sure I know it. She answers my calls to get a diaper change with a resounding "No", my attempts to get her dressed with a pathetically plaintive "Mommy", and if I dare to pick her up to help expedite matters, she becomes as slippery as a lizard, bending her body backwards and shrieking all the while. After she has had her angry say, she cries in a broken-hearted way – as if she has lost her best friend and she runs to her best friend for comfort and safety.

This is the morning routine with Cameryn and it has become more intense as Bruin has grown within Jess. She is more vocal now and peppers her ear-piercing cries with words, some recognizable, some not so. The pattern continues with Mom.

She tries to ignore Cameryn, but it is hard for any mom to ignore her child's broken-hearted sob and Cameryn is a persistent little devil. Mom invariably picks her up, whispers in her ear, dries her tears and helps her blow her nose. I vacillate between backing off and prying Cameryn off Mom so she can work.

I do not listen much to the conversation, but I imagine Mom is saying something like, "Yes my poor dear girl, you have to go with Gloo. I know it is no fun and someday maybe I won't have to work and subject you to this experience." As she whispers to Cameryn, Cameryn looks directly at me, narrowing her eyes into little angry slits to let me know exactly who is in charge.

Whatever it is Mom is saying, it is wholly ineffective. Cameryn sits tight on her lap as if glued there. Mom's desk is an attractive nuisance and Cameryn understandably grabs for all of the interesting stuff. In an effort to direct her away from the work in progress, Jess gives up her cell phone so that Cameryn can enjoy her favorite songs, videos, and pictures. If this seems like a losing battle for me, it is. I have no interest in competing with Mom, but the cell phone – well, no one can compete with that, not even Mom. Mom surrenders to the grubby sticky little hands, gives her warnings every few minutes that she has to get back to work and Cameryn has to go with pathetic Gloo, gives her more time and more warnings and ultimately engages in hand to hand combat to get the phone back. This entire scene makes me crazy. I feel ineffective for one and two, I see a little two-year-old ruling two adults who used to be very capable.

There are days when Cameryn tires of this game and chooses to get down on her own and let me help her get ready for the day. On other occasions, I do actually pry her off of her mom, if her mom is in the middle of a meeting or at her wit's end. Mom often has to take over the dressing and preparing for the day as Cameryn outright rejects my efforts. Once we are out of the house, Cameryn snaps into shape. She loves to be out and about and once out, she remembers that.

I do not have quite the same situation at my own house when Crash and Bear come over. When I am "in charge", Mom and Dad are not around, so they have no one to play to. We do socialize with their mom and dad a lot though. Crash behaves quite differently when they are around. He runs around dumping his toys, refusing to pick them up, and being generally difficult. Even happy Bear becomes unhappy when Mom and Dad are in the room. It is only right that the grandkids prefer their parents over their grandparents, but most grandparents don't see the grands as often as we do, which makes me consider limiting the visits with their parents.

Crash is getting to the age where his interactions with others are not as closely monitored. He takes swim lessons and attends ninja classes without a family protector at his side. The other day he told a fellow swimmer his name, "C-r-a-s-h". Well, he spelled it and then said it. The little boy, Zachary, asked him why that was his name. Crash did not really understand the question and so had no words.

I definitely understood the question as I had asked that same question some three and a half years ago when Crash was born. Crash's parents feel they owe no one an explanation for why they made a name the focal point of this beautiful boy's existence and they bristle at the question.

The problem is Crash will get this question and see the quizzical looks long after they are gone. He needs a strategy in response, or maybe he can use his middle name as his first name or maybe we can come up with a catchy little ditty using the many words that rhyme with Crash – like bash, dash, splash, smash, and flash. I will work on that….

In my short tenure as a grandparent, I know exactly what the problem with grandkids is. The problem with grandkids is their parents.

28

Future Present

A GREATER GOOD

Crash lies quietly on the ground, talking to himself and organizing his cars by style, size, and color. Cameryn alternately colors, strolls her baby and jumps on her trampoline. Bear babbles, crawls to and fro, grunting as he goes and smiling whenever he catches an eye. They all have a fire burning within and a life ahead of them.

I watch them navigate the daily challenges that will give them strength and perseverance to meet the next set of challenges. They ask for help when they need it, but for the most part, they either do not need help or do not want the help. I see this as a good thing. No point waiting around for someone to help you.

The grands are learning they have power, power to do and not to do. They are not yet constrained by social norms so having a tantrum in the store is not embarrassing but liberating. They know how to pit Mom against Gloo, scream pitifully and loudly when Gloo approaches – especially if she approaches to prepare for nap time. And they are learning about the power of their bodies to climb, walk, and run and the power of their minds to focus and attend. I find I am a rudder of little vessels, providing some direction as they scale the waves, find their voices, and swim through the sea of their emotions.

I sometimes yearn for the life I had – a job that is satisfying and rewarding and allows me to get out of myself and out of the house.

One of the pluses of teaching is summer vacation. When you are completely exhausted and think you cannot do it anymore, you get a much needed break from the emotional and physical rollercoaster of being with the future eight to ten hours a day. Teaching takes a toll on the spirit and time is sorely needed from one school year to the next to renew that spirit and re-energize for the next group of kids.

Summer arrives now, but summer break does not. My schedule remains the same, days in Oakland with Cameryn and others with Bear peppered with Crash-time when he is not in preschool. I still am not sure how this happened to me and sometimes I feel I should be doing something more with my life. And then there is a phone call, "Gloo, want to walk with us?" or a joyful laugh when I come into the bedroom early in the morning asking, "Is Cameryn here?" or the quick scurry of pudgy arms and legs as I call to Bear. As much as I loved the routine and reward of teaching, I was able to insulate myself from getting too close or too involved with my students. The grands have stumbled upon a hidden chamber of my heart and pried it wide open.

While the grands' lives are ahead of them, most of mine is behind me. Over the past two years I have fretted over what to do next. I am only now realizing that for the past two years I have been doing what is next. My charge is right in front of me – in the form of these grands, the future shining bright on my present.

I have no desire to live my life through them or to steer them on a predesigned course. The magic of a life is finding one's own way and then realizing at some point that there was some kind of illuminated path even if it may have been a winding one. My job now is to spend time with the grands, love them, talk with them, listen to them, accept them for who they are, and provide the opportunity and freedom for them to learn about the world around them. I strive to nurture their feisty, fun-loving spirits, not crush them.

They say kids keep us young. The mirror seems to tell another story so far, but perhaps there is a reset button….

29

GRAND GIFTS

While I joke that the problem with my grandkids is their parents, my children have given me gifts that I can never repay. They have given me the opportunity to be with these little rascals who in turn have graced me with music, fun, and an alternate view of time. The grands fill a room with laughter. "That is funny, Gloo" echoes in my head. Everything is funny – words, facial expressions, Papa, me. Their laughter is infectious, heartwarming, and energizing.

With the grands, I get to enjoy snack several times a day, judgment free. We have snack before and after music, at the park intermittently, and whenever they come to my house. It is ironic that they associate food with me as I am anything but a foodie. But, like the grands, I appreciate the basics like nuts, peanut butter crackers, popcorn, blueberries and grapes. The other day one parent asked me if Crash is diabetic, having observed us ritually eat before and after music class. Nope, I replied, we are just snacking because we can.

The grands have renewed my love of music. Crash's favorite song for a long time was the song from Madagascar, *I Like to Move It*. The first time we heard it together, we just started moving, of course. We danced through the entire upbeat song. It tired us out for sure and after any rendition of this song now, Crash always says, "This song really makes us tired, Gloo. Let's do the robot now." He has added other songs to his repertoire since then, like Queen's *We Will Rock You*.

Cameryn's favorite right now is *Trot Ole Joe*. I sometimes feel if I hear it one more time, my head is going to explode and yet I play it over and over again. The choice in an enclosed space like a car is a screaming child or an exploding head: I donate my head to the cause. Cameryn loves to dance and any song will get her hopping and skipping and twirling if it catches her ear. Bear too loves to dance and reacts almost immediately to music. He is a big body so the rhythm of the song moves slowly in waves from his head to his toes.

My piano has become a focal point of our home again. I took piano lessons when I was young and I loved playing. My husband bought the piano for me when I was thirty-three, once we had settled on a house to raise our children. I am not impressed by gifts of any sort generally but I was oh so grateful to receive this one.

When my kids were little, I had a rule that they could not interrupt me in the middle of a song. That was fine with Kristen, just keep playing Mom and leave me alone she seemed to say, but Sean would stand next to the piano seemingly vibrating with every note played waiting for the opportunity to tell me the very important thing he had to say. That rule has gone by the wayside.

The grands interrupt all the time – not only do they interrupt but if they had it their way, they would just get up on the bench and sweep me off. It is interesting to see how they manage at the piano. Crash began by banging his flat outstretched hands on the piano keys. When he learned high from low, he played those notes, one high and then one low, repeatedly. Bear has followed in his brother's footsteps and likes to rap on the keys with his pudgy hands. The first time Cameryn sat at the piano, at 12 months or so, she held her hands with unusually good technique, wrists up, fingers extended and slightly bent and spread over the keys as if she had played for years, pressing a single key at a time. She continues to approach the piano as if a concert pianist resides within.

The grands have tapped into the playful side of me and brought it out for all to see. We sing and dance at music class. It felt a little awkward at first to prance about but the grands encouraged me to loosen up the shackles of my adult self. I also enjoy (sort of) the swings, the climbing structures and the slides when we go to the park, although my knees and hips sometimes complain. The grands insist on watching a grown adult play on child-sized stuff — who is in charge of whom, I sometimes wonder.

The grands love to play in front of the two wall-length mirrored closet doors in our master bathroom, enamored with the double images of themselves. They make funny faces, smile, squish their faces into the mirror and mimic their parents. As we play, I cannot avoid the mirror. Thanks to them, I have developed a certain comfort level with the image looking back at me and am more accepting of what I see.

I always viewed time as a measure of what I could accomplish. With each passing year, my mornings begin earlier and earlier. I get up at 3:30 now, which many would say is the middle of the night. I am at the pool a good ten minutes before it opens (4:30 in the morning), hoping to get my preferred lane. It is ridiculous really as more often than not, I am the first one in the pool and sometimes the only one.

As a teacher, I pushed through the curriculum faster each year. I felt the kids were more engaged if I did not beat them with repetition and slow instruction. In retrospect, I see they were victims of my obsession with time.

There is a heightened anxiety that such a mentality engenders. Unfortunately, my children were victims of my rush to beat time. Time has slowed down tremendously in the age of the grands. If they have to get to school or swim class, I am happy to take them but there is no hurry in me. They may take an hour to have breakfast or five minutes. In any event they will not be rushed or someone will pay. I do not want to be the one to pay (a benefit to being Gloo) so I have adjusted my expectations tremendously.

The grands have given me the opportunity to enjoy the passage of time without competing with it. They have added to my life in ways

Jeanne M. Carroll

I cannot possibly measure, filling my heart and soul and helping me to grow into Gloo. With baby Bruin on the way, I am feeling an eerie sense of deja vu, kind of like I am a kid again playing the game of tag. Instead of a fleeting tap on the back and the familiar refrain "tag you're it", I feel a tug deep within my heart and hear a gleeful impish voice exclaim, *"Glooed again!"*

Appendix

A RECIPE FOR A
GRAND LIFE

Over the years, I have baked a lot of sweet things (brownies, cookies, cupcakes, banana bread) but I could not have done it without a recipe. I am not freewheeling when it comes to baking and, as it turns out, I have not been that freewheeling when it comes to living either. While everyone has to find their own way, I think there are a few key ingredients that may help to build a grand life.

Work Hard: Nothing comes to those who sit, watch, and wait. Work hard at everything you do, finish what you start, and do so with your best effort.

Do It Yourself: If something needs to be done, do it. Don't wait for someone else to make your bed, take out the garbage, mow the lawn, clean the house, build your life. Be independent in spirit and in action.

Do what is right: This may be as simple as being accepting of others, especially when others are not, refusing to join in mean-spirited behavior like calling people names, or just saying "no". Heed that little voice in your head that helps you to distinguish right from wrong. When I was in high school, I let a friend of mine drive home drunk. I should have had her spend the night at my house but I was afraid of what my parents would say. My friend lived through that night with some cuts, bruises, a broken cheekbone, and a totaled car. Her parents found her on the floor in their hallway foyer early the next morning. I was not much of a friend – and that night our not-much-of-a-friendship ended. Letting her drive away that night remains one of my greatest disappointments in myself.

Move: The human body is meant to move. That little pump called the heart beats over 2 billion times in a lifetime. The stronger it is, the more we can count on it, but it needs to be worked. So dance, run, swim, lift weights, garden, ride bikes, play sports – anything that is active – just be sure to MOVE it!

Save Your Pennies: Make a purchase only if you have the money to pay for it. Think twice before buying, give yourself a two-week window to consider if you really need that tattoo or the skinny jeans with holes in the knees. *You do not need everything you want.* Delayed gratification will buy you more in the end.

Be You: As you grow up, you will explore who you are. You may want to do what others do, dress like others dress, talk like others talk. No one really escapes peer pressure, but if you do not fit into the generic mold of those around you, do not fret. Rejoice! Your individuality is what makes you special. Stay true to you always.

Take Care of Your Brain: This one little organ uses approximately 20% of our oxygen supply, but is only two percent of our body weight. It makes us who we are, stores all of our precious memories, and controls vital functions of the body. Everything we put into our body affects the brain. Drugs, alcohol, all things foreign to the body can affect the precise operation of the brain, change its nature and therefore change a person's nature. Take care of your brain and it will take care of you.

Be Nice: My mother was a busy lady. Eight kids consumed her time. She had very little advice for me, maybe none at all except for the three words that still echo in my head: "Be Nice Jeannie." This was her usual refrain when I would torment my sister Jill. It is simple, but solid advice for dealing with all who cross our paths.

Look for the Good: There will be plenty of disappointments in life. The key to dealing with them is to stay positive and be resilient. And smile − it costs nothing, is universally understood, and adds a little sunshine to the day.

Say Thank You: People serve us all the time, delivery people, hairdressers, grocery clerks, custodians, doctors, nurses, gardeners, waiters and waitresses. Thank them for their efforts. Don't forget the ones you love and who love you back, the ones who are there for you always. Thank them for helping you with your homework, cleaning the house, stocking the kitchen with food, putting up with your surly attitude, loving you even when you are not loveable. Someday they will be gone from your physical lives, living within the spaces of your thoughts. You can be sure they will be smiling at and with you, and you should have no regrets about what was left unsaid.

Jeanne Carroll grew up in New England, the fourth of eight children. At 21, she escaped to the West Coast, met her husband to whom she has been married for forty years and with whom she raised two children, and spent the better part of her life trying to harness her energy in a productive way. Jeanne majored in Biology, worked in toxicology for four years, attended law school, and practiced law for fourteen years. At the ripe age of 42, she obtained her teaching credential and for the next 19 years taught Physical Science to middle school students. Her greatest challenge was giving up work, retiring, and taking on the care of lively, lovely, and sometimes obstinate grandchildren.

Glooed is Jeanne's first book. Jeanne teamed with her sister, Deb Risotti, to write *Sarah's World*, a book that chronicles the incredible life of Deb's daughter through her 24 years. Despite suffering a devastating brain injury during the course of her birth, Sarah touched the lives of all who met her. Jeanne was able to help Deb put her heart and soul on paper because in some small but very significant way, Jeanne felt what Deb lived, a phenomenon arising from their shared sibling experience.

Jeanne can be reached at Glooed54@gmail.com.

www.ingramcontent.com/pod-product-compliance
Lightning Source LLC
Chambersburg PA
CBHW060512280326
41933CB00014B/2940